Responding
to the
Call of Ministry

REVEREND ALICE J. DISE

A STUDY MANUAL AND
WORKBOOK FOR MINISTERS

FOREWORD BY ALVIN LEWIS, PH.D., M.DIV.

Copyright © 2004 by Reverend Alice J. Dise
2nd Edition 2009
3rd Edition 2020
All rights reserved.

No part of this book may be reproduced in any form or by any means, electronic or mechanical, including photocopying, recording, video, or by any information or retrieval system, without prior written permission from the publisher except for the use of brief quotations in a book review.

Published in the United States by Uriel Press, a division of UMI
P.O. Box 436987, Chicago, IL 60643
www.urielpress.com
ISBN: 978-0-9993326-8-9 (paperback)

All scripture quotations, unless otherwise indicated, are taken from the "Holy Bible, New International Version – NIV" (International Bible Society), or Holy Bible King James Version – KJV (Thomas Nelson Publishers).

Cover Design & Book Design: Kimberly Applewhite

Printed in the United States of America.

Dedication

To my husband, "Bill," who has encouraged me so many times, in so many ways, from the beginning of this project until its completion. And to my oldest daughter Ivy who won't allow me to stop working. I greatly appreciate her help with compiling and editing the third edition.

To my pastor, Rev. Jerald January Sr., and the ministerial team at Vernon Park Church of God, where I serve as Body Life Pastor and director of the Minister's Assembly. You have been my prayer support and my "sounding board." Our studies and conclusions together make up the basis for this book.

To my ministerial students at the In-Service Training Institute of the National Association of the Church of God (I.S.T.I.) held at Anderson University in 2001. You were among the first groups with whom I used some of the material. Thank you for refusing to accept my excuses to stop the project. Your insistence that I complete the book remained with me until I did so.

Finally, to my mom, Evangelist Mary Wilson, whose story is told in this book, and whose dedication to God and ministry has been my inspiration for more than half a century. She passed away in 1951, but the words from one of her sermons, "We Ought to Obey God Rather than Men," still resound in my spirit.

Foreword

Rev. Alice Dise has written a resourceful book that will prove helpful to the experienced or newly called minister/pastor. This publication can really be described as a teaching manual, or workbook, for conducting effective ministry in a local congregation. The manual is divided into the following five parts:

The Call to Ministry
The Call to Commitment
Understanding the Worship Experience
Understanding Corporate Worship
The Ministry at Work

Each section is intended to help the minister/pastor reflect on and contemplate the concerns and content of what ministry is all about. The aspiring minister and seasoned pastor alike will find this workbook to be both didactic and diagnostic in relating the content to the reader. The majority of the material contained in this manual invites the reader to explore, interact, and evaluate his or her ministerial call, commitment, and understanding regarding ministry. As one reads through the biblical content and the quotations from the different cited writers, the reader is challenged to answer a series of questions and follow the instructions in each of the five parts.

Rev. Dise writes as a well-seasoned and established minister of the Gospel, who knows and understands clearly what it means to be a fully functioning minister. For example, it is quite apparent as one explores this resource that she writes with commanding authority about the essence of the practical side of ministry. Rev. Dise, therefore, writes as a coach and a counselor giving directions and principles for persons engaged in ministerial service.

It is also obvious that Rev. Dise's experience radiates strongly as the body life pastor of a growing and thriving congregation, along with her many years of service as an associate minister and preacher of the Gospel. In my opinion, Rev. Dise's work provides ministers with the help they need to enhance their ministry to the church. As I read through this manual, I was greatly benefited and wished that I'd had such a book when I began my ministry nearly 50 years ago! As a senior pastor, I will strongly urge my ministerial staff to read and study this manual.

Rev. Dise is to be commended for her creative style of writing and the important contribution she has made to those men and women who seek to enrich their personal lives and ministries.

Alvin Lewis, Ph.D., M.Div.
Senior Pastor
Central Community Church of God
Jackson, MS—2004

Contents

PREFACE	VIII
INTRODUCTION	IX
TOOLS AND RESOURCES FOR THIS STUDY GUIDE	X

PART ONE: THE CALL OF MINISTRY

Developing the Minister's Affirmation	3
The Call to Serve	5
The "Call"—What Does It Mean?	7
The Source, the Service, the Specialty	15

PART TWO: THE CALL TO COMMITMENT

The Call to Commitment	21
God's Promises to Those He Calls for Service	30
God, Answer Me Please!	33
Disciplines Required to Become an Effective Minister	37
Questionnaire for Ministers Seeking Credentials	46

PART THREE: UNDERSTANDING THE WORSHIP EXPERIENCE

Understanding Worship	53
How Does One Worship?	55
God, the Object of Our Worship	56

PART FOUR: UNDERSTANDING CORPORATE WORSHIP

Leading the Church in Worship	61
Understanding the Segments of the Worship Service	64
Glossary of Terms for Leading the Worship Service	72
The Call to Corporate Praise	76
The Call to Corporate Prayer	79
The Call to Corporate Proclamation	82
The Call to Corporate Response (the Altar)	84
A Service of Celebration—The Lord's Supper	100

PART FIVE: THE MINISTRY AT WORK

Dos and Don'ts When Visiting the Sick	104
What Must I Do to Be Saved? (Leading Someone to Christ)	107
The Gravesite Ceremony	110
House Calls to the Bereaved	112
Biblical Foundations of Marriage	114

Preface

Luke 4:18–19 gives an account of Jesus in the synagogue (place of worship). He was given a book. He opened it and read from the book of the prophet Esaias:

> *"The Spirit of the Lord is upon me, because he hath anointed me to preach the gospel to the poor; he hath sent me to heal the brokenhearted, to preach deliverance to the captives, and recovering of sight to the blind, to set at liberty them that are bruised, To preach the acceptable year of the Lord."*

Completing the reading, Jesus closed the book, returned it to the minister, and took His seat. As all eyes were fastened on Him, He said,

> *"This day is this scripture fulfilled in your ears"* (from Luke 4:21, KJV).

As each minister goes forth, he or she must continue the legacy left by our Lord of preaching, healing, and the releasing of captives. Our works must bear witness to the indwelling of the Holy Spirit and the anointing for ministry to which we have been called.

To that end, this book is dedicated.

Rev. Alice J. Dise.

Introduction

This book was born as a result of requests from numerous people who attended the classes from which the content came. These classes, held at conferences, workshops, and even my home church, Vernon Park Church of God in Chicago, Illinois, proved to be helpful to ministers, ministers in training, deacons, and other church leaders. It is especially intended to help new ministers, and in some cases, even seasoned ministers to:

1. Understand their call to ministry.

2. Provide information that will enable new ministers to begin honing their ministry skills in their respective congregations while pursuing further study.

3. Address the many unanswered questions that arise during ministry service, thereby helping to conquer fears both real and imagined.

This guide is not intended to be a replacement for theological study. It deals primarily with the how to's of serving in various facets of ministry. With this book, ministers will be able to participate comfortably in on the job training.

This manual is suitable for independent self-paced study or for groups. Each section contains reflections and exercises intended to reinforce the learning. Discussing your answers to the exercises with mentors and others will deepen and expand your thinking on the various topics.

Tools and Resources for this Study Guide

The following is a list of materials that will be useful for studying in this manual. In fact no minister's "arsenal" is complete without one or more examples of each of these tools. All are available in print and online.

1. **A Bible**

    I refer to the King James Version in this manual. But new ministers should become familiar with several versions, especially what is used by your church and denomination. Any Bible that you prefer can be used with the reflections and most exercises in this book.

2. **A Concordance**

    A biblical concordance is used to find scriptures related to a specific topic or idea. I use the New American Standard Exhaustive Concordance (by Robert L. Thomas), but there are many tools for this purpose.

3. **A Biblical Commentary**

    These tools provide analysis and interpretation of the scriptures based upon the historical and scholarly contexts. The Wesleyan Bible Commentary and the Wycliffe Commentary are traditional resources widely used by ministers and others to study the Bible. However culturally specific commentary (for example, "Stony the Road We Trod: An African-American Biblical Interpretation", by Cain Hope Felder) and other modern day explanations of the Bible also exist.

4. **A Bible Dictionary**

    This is an absolute necessity to understand unfamiliar Biblical words and phrases.

5. **Collections of Sermons**

   Reading sermons from other ministers provides inspiration, ideas, and examples. Obtain them in books, recordings, and directly from preachers you admire.

6. **Ministers Manual or Handbook**

   These provide references and preparation aides for church services and religious events. I use Special Occasions in the Black Church (by Benjamin Stanley Baker), the Star Book for Ministers, (by Edward T. Hiscox), and several other manuals.

7. **Church Doctrine**

   Collect all documents that explain and discuss your doctrine, beliefs, and church tenets.

Part One:
The Call of Ministry

"So do not be ashamed to testify about our Lord, or ashamed of me his prisoner. But join with me in suffering for the gospel, by the power of God."
(2 Timothy 1:8, NIV)

"The Spirit of the Lord is on me, because he has anointed me to preach good news to the poor. He has sent me to proclaim feedom for the prisoners and recovery of sight for the blind, to release the oppressed, to proclaim the year of the Lord's favor."

(Luke 4:18–19, NIV)

THE CALL OF MINISTRY

DEVELOPING THE MINISTER'S AFFIRMATION

Using Luke 4:18–19, take a few minutes to fill in the blank spaces. Put an X beside those areas that apply to you.

"It is GOD who has sent me, _____."
write your name

HE...

( ) has ANOINTED

( ) has SENT

me, _____
write your name

( ) to PREACH GOOD NEWS

to _____

FREEDOM for the prisoners

( ) to PROCLAIM

RECOVERY of sight

for _____

( ) to RELEASE

THE _____

THE MINISTER'S AFFIRMATION

Effective ministry can only be achieved when one realizes the call of God. Luke 4:18–19 provides the basis for the minister's affirmation.

It is **GOD** who has called **ME** to ministry.

GOD'S anointing upon my life is enabling **ME** to minister.

GOD'S power will prevail whenever, wherever,

and to whomever **GOD** sends **ME** to minister.

Repeat this affirmation often! It will help to keep you focused and encouraged. Remember, effective ministry can only be realized when one realizes the call of God upon his or her life.

THE CALL OF MINISTRY

THE CALL TO SERVE

"…But whosoever will be great among you, shall be your minister: and whosoever of you will be the chiefest, shall be servant of all" (Mark 10:43–44, KJV).

Minister: *Diakonos* (Gr.)—a servant; one who serves the church as pastor, assistant, associate, or leader of a special ministry (e.g., youth, Christian education, music, etc.) on a full-time or part-time basis.

Despite the many directions or courses of action that the call to ministry can take in a person's life, it is clear that ministry is about serving. Whether in the pulpit as a prophet or priest, in the pews, or beyond the walls of the sanctuary, the fact is, a minister is called to serve. Ever since Jesus called a group of followers to become "fishers of men," thousands of men and women have answered the call to serve and become ministers of the Gospel of Jesus Christ.

The ministry gifts are varied, but the primary focus of all Christian ministry is salvation and bringing men, women, boys, and girls to the knowledge and acceptance of Jesus Christ as Savior.

Just as those who were called by Jesus were from various backgrounds and walks of life, the same continues to be true today. Each person called into ministry is uniquely gifted and talented to fulfill God's call in his or her own way. Age is not a factor. Some are called at a very young age, while others are much older and heed the call after many years of church attendance. Some even choose ministry as a second career. In fact, *Parade* magazine reported that "at least half of all the men and women entering seminaries today to become priests, ministers or rabbis are over the age of 35 and have sacrificed successful careers and prosperous lifestyles."

THE CALL OF MINISTRY

REFLECTIONS

1. Write the Minister's Affirmation in the space provided below. Affirm it in your heart today—keeping in mind the key words: GOD and ME.

_____
_____
_____
_____
_____
_____
_____

2. Fill in the blank space below:

One who serves people in response to God's call is a

_____
_____
_____
_____
_____
_____
_____

THE CALL OF MINISTRY

THE "CALL"—WHAT DOES IT MEAN?

What is it that brings people to ministry? Many people who've been asked this question simply respond—"a call."

What is a "call" to ministry?
Ministry has been described as an inner compulsion—a drive—which makes you feel obliged to respond. This inner compulsion is fueled with the assurance that God has designated ministry as one's divine purpose. One woman responded by saying, "it was what my heart was calling me to do." For many, the *call* has come quietly, to the extent that they cannot pinpoint the exact time they heard God's voice. For others, the *call* to ministry was more dramatic and came in the form of a dream or a vision. But one thing is certain, even though the *call* to ministry may come in many different forms, the inner compulsion—the drive—is real, and those who are called into ministry know it.

Martin Luther King Sr., the father of late civil rights leader, Dr. Martin Luther King Jr., once said that *"one knows that he has been called to preach when he cannot help himself—he cannot stop preaching."* His words bear out the prophet Jeremiah, who said:

> *"...His word was in mine heart as a burning fire shut up in my bones..."*
> (from Jeremiah 20:9, KJV).

Whatever area of ministry one is called to serve in, the inner compulsion to fulfill the call is no less significant. It is based on the firm belief that one's desire to serve is rooted in the desire to please God. Take, for example, Corrie Ten Boom. Carole Carlson tells the story of Corrie Ten Boom, a noted female Dutch minister who became famous during World War II for her work and ministry in the Nazi concentration camps. As the story goes, Corrie was told by a visiting American from Harlem, "It's not easy to make one's way to America." Corrie responded by saying, *"I believe you, but God has directed me, and I must obey."*

The Call of Ministry

In another instance, Stephanie Graham in her work *Faith Power* also summarizes the feelings of others called to serve in ministry:

> *"This gift of faith...has guided me as I have journeyed through racist religious institutions...It guides me when I am faced with the seduction of power, privilege and prestige...In that quiet place I am reminded of my role in my family, in my ministry, and in my relationship with God. I am reminded that the battle is not mine, that it belongs to the Lord. For whatever reason, the Lord has chosen to use me as a vessel to accomplish a part of God's agenda. Mine is not an uncommon story."* [3]

To understand the various ways in which people experience God's call, let's look at several examples.

Jeremiah

"The word of the Lord came to me saying, 'Before I formed you in the womb I knew you, before you were born I set you apart; I appointed you as a prophet to the nations.' 'Ah, Sovereign Lord,' I said, 'I do not know how to speak; I am only a child.' But the Lord said to me, 'Do not say, "I am only a child." You must go to everyone I send you to and say whatever I command you'" (Jeremiah 1:4–7).

Jeremiah was given a difficult assignment. Neither his position nor his assignment was negotiable. As a prophet, he received a divine call to warn all the people—kings, princes, and the commoner—regarding God's pending judgment because of their sins of idolatry. God warned Jeremiah of the difficulty that he would face, but assured him of His presence and ultimate deliverance (see Jeremiah 1:10, 16, 18).

Jeremiah's words do not explain how or in what way the word of the Lord came to him, whether in a dream, a vision, or in his spirit. But it is clear from this reference, as well as others, that Jeremiah is convinced he received prophetic inspiration from the Lord.

1. What, if anything, is unique about Jeremiah's calling?

_____

_____

THE CALL OF MINISTRY

2. List the difficulties Jeremiah faced before he began to minister.

_____

_____

_____

3. What do you think may have been Jeremiah's inspiration to obey God?

_____

_____

_____

Evangelist Mary Adams Wilson (a 20th century evangelist)

Mary Adams Wilson often defended her call to ministry by telling of numerous dreams that she had in which she was preaching. She could repeat the details of the dreams with precision whenever asked to do so. Despite opposition from her husband and other family members who were uncomfortable with women preachers, she was convinced of her calling. Her ministry took her to the county jail to preach to inmates, to hospitals to pray and minister to the sick, and to the streets in street ministry. Wherever there was an opportunity to share the call God had placed within her heart, Mary was there.

Evangelist Wilson's ministry transpired during a time when women in ministerial roles were not too popular, particularly in the Baptist church. Many who knew Mary said that she exhibited a "sense of urgency" for the Gospel that could not be discouraged by friend or foe. A portion of a poem she penned presents a good picture of her intentions regarding ministry.

"When I remember the days of old,
And meditate on thy works,
I pray…Dear God,
Help me to work day by day
and never my duty to shirk."

THE CALL OF MINISTRY

1. What, if anything, was unique about Evangelist Wilson's calling?"

_____
_____
_____

2. List some of the difficulties she overcame in order to fulfill her ministerial call.

_____
_____
_____

3. In your opinion, what inspired Evangelist Wilson to continue ministering in an environment that was particularly unpopular for women?

_____
_____
_____

The Apostle Paul

At the time of Paul's encounter with the Lord, he was on a mission as a strong believer and proponent of the Jewish faith. Once called to Christian ministry, he expended the same kind of enthusiasm and energy that had characterized his previous activities.

In the following passage of Scripture, Paul presents his case before Herod Agrippa:

"About noon, O king, as I was on the road, I saw a light from heaven, brighter than the sun, blazing around me and my companions. We all fell to the ground, and I heard a voice saying to me in Aramaic, 'Saul, Saul, why do you persecute me? It is hard for you to kick against the goads.' Then I asked, 'Who are you, Lord?' 'I am Jesus, whom you are persecuting,' the Lord replied. 'Now get up and stand on your feet. I have appeared to you to appoint you as a servant and as a witness of what you have seen of me and what I will show you. I will rescue you from your own people and from the Gentiles. I am sending you to them, to open their eyes and

THE CALL OF MINISTRY

turn them from darkness to light, and from the power of Satan to God, so that they may receive forgiveness of sins and place among those who are sanctified by faith in me'" (Acts 26:13–18, NIV).

Paul's work caused him a great deal of suffering from which he never reneged (see 2 Corinthians 11:23–31). He is quoted as having said to Timothy, his son in the ministry, "I have fought a good fight, I have finished my course, I have kept the faith" (2 Timothy 4:7, NIV).

1. What is unique about Paul's calling?

_____
_____
_____

2. What kind of difficulties did Paul face when God called him to ministry?

_____
_____
_____

3. What do you think inspired Paul to obey God's call despite the many difficulties he faced?

_____
_____
_____

Simon & Andrew

"As Jesus was walking beside the Sea of Galilee, he saw two brothers, Simon called Peter and his brother Andrew. They were casting a net into the lake, for they were fisherman. 'Come, follow me,' Jesus said, 'and I will make you fishers of men.' At once they left their nets and followed him" (Matthew 4:18–20, NIV).

Jesus could tell that brothers Simon and Andrew were good at their profession. So much so that He invited them to follow Him and become fishers of men.

The Call of Ministry

The call of Simon and Andrew was two-fold: *"Come, follow me,"* and *"Become fishers of men."* Both men responded immediately by leaving their nets behind. Both also spent a great deal of time in the company of Jesus observing what He did and what He said.

Not too much is known of Andrew's ministry separate from the Twelve. However, we do know that Simon (later named Peter) was impetuous and fearful and had a lot to learn. The first thing Simon Peter had to learn was self-control.

One day Peter became angry and cut off the ear of the high priest's servant Malchus in an attempt to protect Jesus from being taken by soldiers. Jesus, expressing his disapproval of Peter's action, told him to put his sword away (John 18:10–11). On another occasion, Peter denied even knowing Jesus (John 18:17, 25, 27). Nevertheless, Peter was among the first to arrive at the sepulcher when Mary Magdalene told him the tomb was empty, fearing someone had stolen Jesus' body.

Peter quickly learned the true meaning of forgiveness when Jesus appeared to him and the disciples on the shore after His resurrection (ref. John 21). On the day of Pentecost it was Peter who served as spokesperson for the disciples. He knew of Joel's prophecies and could explain to all who inquired as to the meaning of the events of the day (Acts 2:14). Even amid criticism and threats, Peter prayed for boldness to speak God's Word. He considered himself blessed that he was among the "worthy" who would suffer for the name of Jesus (Acts 5:41).

1. What is unique about the "call" of Simon Peter and Andrew?

_____
_____
_____
_____
_____
_____

The Call of Ministry

2. Give examples of possible difficulties Simon Peter and Andrew faced when changing vocations.

_____
_____
_____
_____
_____
_____
_____

3. What do you think prompted Simon Peter and Andrew to continue their pursuit of God's call?

_____
_____
_____
_____
_____
_____
_____

THE CALL OF MINISTRY

REFLECTIONS

1. List at least three common elements for all the ministries discussed in this section.

    a. _____

    _____

    b. _____

    _____

    c. _____

    _____

2. Of the individuals discussed, which call to ministry most closely resembles your personal call to ministry? In what way?

_____

_____

_____

_____

_____

_____

_____

THE CALL OF MINISTRY

THE SOURCE, THE SERVICE, THE SPECIALTY

The assurance that God has called you coupled with the inner compulsion to serve, one might find himself or herself faced with the question: *"Where do we go from here?"* Well, the new minister (or even the seasoned minister) must always remember:

A. The Source
B. The Service
C. The Specialty

The Source

God is the source of your call.
The Bible says that Samuel heard a voice calling his name. It was not until he had heard the call three times and Eli the priest confirmed that it was God's voice he heard, that Samuel was convinced of God's calling him.

> *"The Lord called Samuel a third time, and Samuel got up and went to Eli and said, "Here, I am; you called me." Then Eli realized that the Lord was calling the boy. So Eli told Samuel, "Go and lie down, and if he calls you, say, 'Speak, LORD, for your servant is listening.' So Samuel went and lay down in his place. The LORD came and stood there, calling as at the other times, 'Samuel! Samuel!' Then Samuel said, 'Speak, for your servant is listening'"* (1 Samuel 3:8–10, NIV).

Samuel's first assignment would involve him telling of the impending doom against Eli's house (1 Samuel 3:11–14).

Imagine having to tell the priest about God's displeasure with his actions! Certainly, knowing it was God (and not Eli) who he would have to answer to made a difference.

The Call of Ministry

The Service

God calls ministers to service.

Jesus said:

> *"...whoever wants to become great among you must be your servant...For even the Son of Man did not come to be served, but to serve, and to give his life as a ransom for many"* (Mark 10:43, 45, NIV).

Both James and Paul spoke of themselves as servants.

> True servants:
> - Give of themselves.
> - Are accountable to an owner or employer.
> - Have a job or responsibility.

The Specialty

It is God who determines the area of ministry in which you serve based on the talents and gifts He has provided to you.

Do not be limited by what you think you can (or cannot) do; rather, be open to study and learn. Even though your gifts and talents may be apparent, the minister should seek God earnestly through prayer and fasting to know the area of ministry to which he or she has been called.

> *"And he gave some, apostles; and some, prophets; and some, evangelists; and some, pastors and teachers"* (Ephesians 4:11, KJV).

Dr. Cheryl J. Sanders, senior pastor of the Third Street Church of God in Washington, D.C., grew up in the church that she now pastors. In addition to being a pastor, she taught at Howard University and has authored many religious and scholarly works.

The Call of Ministry

Dr. Sanders knows the meaning of service and gives this advice to individuals contemplating ministry service:

"With God's grace, you can make it through the criticisms and opposition that come from time to time."

Don't be fearful (2 Timothy 1:7).
Do your best (Matthew 25:20–21).
Know that God has promised to be with you (Matthew 28:19–20).
Be strong in the Lord and the power of His might (Ephesians 6:10).

PART TWO:
The Call to Commitment

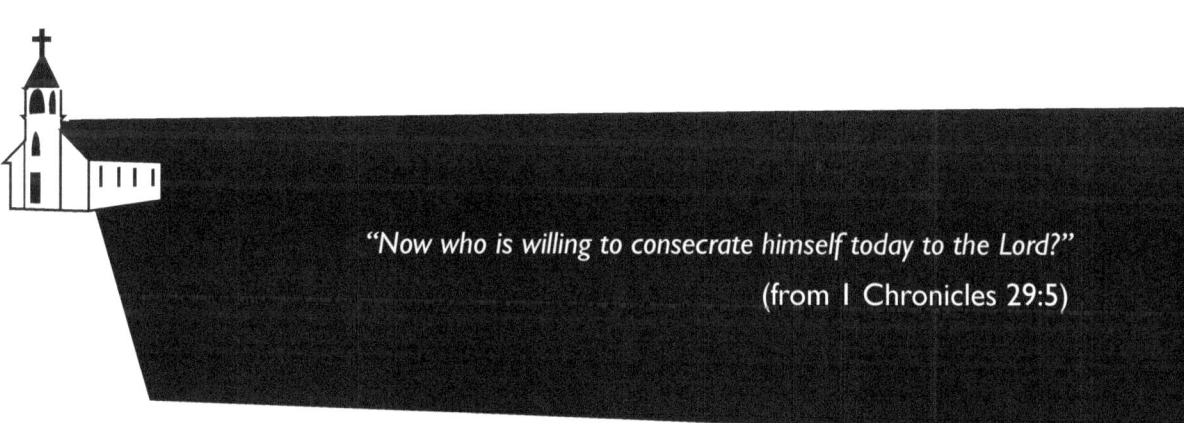

"Now who is willing to consecrate himself today to the Lord?"

(from 1 Chronicles 29:5)

"Then I heard the voice of the Lord saying, 'Whom shall I send? And who will go for us?' And I said, 'Here am I. Send me!'"

(Isaiah 6:8, NIV)

THE CALL TO COMMITMENT

Calling is what God does. Commitment is what people do in response to God's call in order to fulfill the obligations of ministry. To make a meaningful commitment, one must consider the following:

Commitment requires acceptance.

The first challenge of ministry is acceptance by saying yes to God's call. Do not think it strange that you have had to struggle with the decision to become a minister. Contrary to what many believe, people do not readily choose to become ministers. For many, the decision to commit to God's call took many long hours alone with God in prayer—in a private Gethsemane—before coming to the decision to commit to service.

Commitment requires acknowledgment.

The sooner you acknowledge your call (to yourself and others), the sooner you will be on your way to discovering God's plan for your ministry. First you need to tell your family, your spouse, and your friends about your decision. You may also want to speak with another minister, perhaps someone who is following a similar path in ministry as the one you've chosen. Have a talk with your pastor. Don't be put off by those with negative or pessimistic views. People may not believe you immediately, but if you are true and faithful to your calling they will become convinced over time.

Commitment requires counting up the cost.

Prayerfully take an appraisal of what the call to ministry will require of you. In other words, count up the cost. Ministry is hard work. It is characterized by one's faith, confidence in God, steadfastness, unwavering pursuit of purpose, and hard work that requires action with a dedicated effort.

THE CALL TO COMMITMENT

Luke put it this way:

"Suppose one of you wants to build a tower. Will he not first sit down and estimate the cost to see if he has enough money to complete it?" (Luke 14:28, NIV).

Commitment requires preparation of the inner-self.

In Ephesians 3, Paul gives a four-fold revelation about the effects of preparing one's inner-self.

> "I pray that out of his glorious riches he may strengthen you with power through his Spirit in your inner being, so that... (v. 16)
>
> - Christ may dwell in your hearts through faith (v. 17).
> - [You] may have power, together with all the saints, to grasp how wide and long and high and deep is the love of Christ (v. 18).
> - [You] know this love that surpasses knowledge (from v. 19).
> - [You] may be filled to the measure of all the fullness of God" (NIV).

The inner person is sustained through a disciplined prayer life in conjunction with the systematic reading and meditating of the Word of God. Such dedicated time in the Word serves as preparation time for ministry. God must be allowed to speak to the minister before he or she can effectively minister to others.

Most important to a minister's successful development is a devoted prayer life that keeps him or her in touch with the source of their faith—Jesus.

Commitment requires discipline.

The first lesson a minister needs to learn is discipline. Having a disciplined prayer life and enough discipline to systematically read, study, and meditate on God's Word (for the benefit of themselves and others) is a threefold process; it requires **purpose**, **effort**, and **time**.

THE CALL TO COMMITMENT

Purpose—The minister's purpose is to serve effectively by reaching people for Christ and convincing them of His saving grace. Thus, having a clearly defined purpose allows for the release of the spiritual elements essential for a successful ministry.

> *"…because our gospel came to you not simply with words, but also with power, with the Holy Spirit and with deep conviction"* (from 1 Thessalonians 1:5, NIV).

When the mandate was given, Christ made the purpose clear:

> *"All authority in heaven and on earth has been given to me…Therefore go and make disciples of all nations…teaching them to obey everything I have commanded you"* (from Matthew 28:18–20, NIV).

Effort—Purposeful ministry also requires great effort. Because there are so many distractions in ministry, both personal and otherwise, a deliberate effort is necessary to bring the mind and the spirit together as one under the subjection of God's will that requires an effective prayer life. A good prayer with which to begin your devotional period is, *"Let the words of my mouth, and the meditation of my heart, be acceptable in thy sight, O LORD, my strength, and my redeemer"* (Psalm 19:14, KJV).

Time—The minister who conveys God's Word must first spend time communicating with Him. How much time should be spent in prayer? Obviously, there is no set time limit to the amount of time one spends in prayer. However, those who approach prayer in a hurry are in effect saying they don't have time to talk to or listen to God. I've often heard it said, *"pray until you begin to pray."* Isaiah suggests that *waiting* on the Lord is the key to a good prayer life: *"Blessed are all that wait for him [the Lord]"* (from Isaiah 30:18, KJV). The goal is to wait long enough to receive renewal and to communicate frequently enough to keep the two-way channel of communication open. Paul says it like this, *"…the inward man is renewed day by day"* (from 2 Corinthians 4:16, KJV).

THE CALL TO COMMITMENT

Commitment requires study.

Ministry is a profession as well as a calling. Commitment to ministry, therefore, requires that one prepares to *"...rightly divide the word of truth"* (paraphrased from 2 Timothy 2:15, KJV). The minister must study God's Word for illumination and direction. The Bible is the main source of information. Other historical or philosophical text may be used for life application, but they must line up with the Bible.

> *"Do your best to present yourself to God as one approved, a workman who does not need to be ashamed and who correctly handles the word of truth"* (2 Timothy 2:15, NIV).

Commitment requires action.

Ministry requires work and work implies action. That means, in ministry, as in life, you do what you do in obedience to God, the one who gives you the action plan.

> *"See to it that you complete the work you have received in the Lord"* (from Colossians 4:17, NIV).

THE CALL TO COMMITMENT

REFLECTIONS

The following questions are intended to help you search for answers regarding your personal call to ministry and determine the level of your personal commitment to God's call. The intent is to help you assess your personal response to God's call by asking why and wherefore you have been called.

Be honest and sincere when reflecting on your answers. Be as specific and detailed as possible and think carefully before you write so that your answers will reflect your true feelings.

Your Personal Call to Ministry

1. What is your definition of ministry?

___

2. At what point did you first feel the call to Christian ministry? What happened?

___

3. To which area of ministry have you been called to serve? Why do you feel this way?

___

THE CALL TO COMMITMENT

4. Summarize your ministry. What specific acts have you recently been involved in that reflect your ministry calling?

_____
_____
_____

5. Who or what has been your greatest influence to answer the call of ministry? How has this person or event affected your decision to answer the call?

_____
_____
_____

6. List what you believe to be your gifts and in what way(s) you believe your gifts will be helpful in your ministry.

Gift(s)	**How you plan to use them in ministry**
_____	_____
_____	_____
_____	_____
_____	_____

7. List several things you believe will hinder your ministry and what plans (if any) you have to eliminate them.

Hinderances	**What I will do to strengthen them**
_____	_____
_____	_____
_____	_____
_____	_____

THE CALL TO COMMITMENT

Your Personal Response to the Call

1. What was your initial response to the call? Receptive? Reluctant? Or filled with mixed emotions? Explain your answer.

_____
_____
_____

2. How do you feel now? Receptive? Reluctant? Mixed emotions? Why?

_____
_____
_____

3. What do you feel is unique about your call to ministry?

_____
_____
_____

Your Personal Commitment

Calling is what God does. Commitment is what people do in response to God's call in order to fulfill the obligations of ministry. Answer the following questions to determine your level of commitment:

1. What activities are you engaged in that demonstrate your commitment to growing your ministry?

_____
_____
_____

THE CALL TO COMMITMENT

2. How much time do you spend studying God's Word, whether in formal study such as in seminary or Bible school, general study as in attending Sunday School or Bible class, or private study?

_____
_____
_____

3. Describe your personal commitment to discipline as it relates to ministry (e.g., purpose, effort, time).

_____
_____
_____

4. How much time are you willing to devote to learning ministry through on-the-job training?

_____
_____
_____

5. In which areas of ministry are you most willing to work (i.e., sick visitations, teaching, youth ministry, other)?

_____
_____
_____

6. In what area of ministry do you believe your gift(s) will be most effective?

_____
_____
_____

THE CALL TO COMMITMENT

7. Which areas of your life would you say require the most improvements to fulfill your ministry call? What are you willing to do about it?

_____
_____
_____

Write a personal prayer for God's help in this area.

_____
_____
_____
_____
_____
_____
_____
_____

Review the Minister's Affirmation and write it below.

_____
_____
_____
_____

Repeat the Minister's Affirmation often; it will help you stay focused.

THE CALL TO COMMITMENT

GOD'S PROMISES TO THOSE HE CALLS FOR SERVICE

Throughout the Bible there are many whom God has called to ministry who lacked the confidence, experience, and knowledge to carry out the call by themselves. But Scripture tells us that *"God is not a man, that he should lie, nor the son of man, that he should change his mind"* (from Numbers 23:19, NIV) because *"…for he who promised is faithful"* (from Hebrews 10:23, NIV).

LEADER	FEARS/OBSTACLES	GOD'S PROMISE
Joshua	Taking another leader's place (Joshua 1:1–2)	"I will not fail thee, nor forsake thee." (from Joshua 1:5, KJV)
Moses	Lacking eloquent speech (Exodus 4:10)	"Now go; I will help you speak and will teach you what to say." (Exodus 4:12, NIV)
James and John	Common people, fishermen (Matthew 4:18)	"…and I will make you fishers of men." (from Matthew 4:19, NIV)
Peter	Slow to apprehend deeper truths (Matthew 15:15–16)	"I will give you the keys of the kingdom of heaven; whatever you bind on earth will be bound in heaven, and whatever you loose on earth will be loosed in heaven." (Matthew 16:19, NIV)
Deborah	A woman in leadership (Judges 4:4–5)	"I will go with you. But because of the way you are going about this, the honor will not be yours, for the LORD will hand Sisera over to a woman." (Judges 4:9)
The Apostles	Doubt and fear (John 14)	"…the Counselor, the Holy Spirit, whom the Father will send in my name, will teach you all things and will remind you of everything I have said to you." (from John 14:26, NIV)
The Seventy	The need for assurance (Luke 10:17)	"I have given you authority to trample on snakes and scorpions and to overcome all the power of the enemy; nothing will harm you." (Luke 10:19, NIV)
Paul	Newly called preacher (Acts 22:1–19)	"Get up…and go into Damascus. There you will be told all that you have been assigned to do." (from Acts 22:10, NIV)
Solomon	A young, inexperienced king (1 Chronicles 29:1)	"Wisdom and knowledge will be given you" (from 2 Chronicles 1:12, NIV)

THE CALL TO COMMITMENT

REFLECTIONS

Based on the table "God's Promises to Those He Calls for Service," list at least five times that Jesus said "I will..." when He spoke about making a promise.

1. _____
2. _____
3. _____
4. _____
5. _____

Match each name in the first column to the promise that God made in the second column. Put an X beside each promise you have personally experienced in your ministry.

The Seventy	power to bind and release
Joshua	saving of souls
Deborah	protection
The Apostles	victory in a woman's name
Moses	an understanding of life
Peter	victory in battle
James and John	deliverance from oppression
Paul	memory restored by the Holy Spirit
Solomon	given directions once in Damascus

THE CALL TO COMMITMENT

God's Promises to Me

Examine your own fears or obstacles and list them below. Then search the Scriptures to find God's promises for you.

FEARS AND OBSTACLES	GOD'S PROMISES FOR ME
_____	_____
_____	_____
_____	_____
_____	_____
_____	_____
_____	_____
_____	_____

The key words in the Minister's Affirmation are GOD and ME. What significance does this have for you and your ministry?

_____
_____
_____
_____
_____
_____

THE CALL TO COMMITMENT

GOD, ANSWER ME PLEASE!

Oftentimes, as one ponders his or her call to ministry, many questions arise. The questions below were the ones most frequently asked by ministers in training. They have been collected from workshops I've conducted over the years. The answers are the result of class discussions or my personal observations.

1. How can I be sure that God has called me to ministry if I haven't had a vision or a dream.

Consider the following as possibilities:

- *The presbyters.* The laying on of hands, or prophetic announcement. Timothy's calling came through the laying on of hands (2 Timothy 1:6).

- *Opportunities.* The Bible teaches that "a man's gift maketh room" (Proverbs 18:16). If an opportunity or need does exist, this may be the confirmation of one's call.

- *Personal passion.* Oftentimes, one's personal passion is probably an indication of one's calling.

2. How do I begin to answer God's call to ministry?

– With acceptance and acknowledgment.

– With preparation, study, and personal preparedness.

– With study, both formal (seminary or Bible college) or informal (Sunday School, Bible classes, and personal private study).

– With prayer and a commitment to prepare the inner-self.

THE CALL TO COMMITMENT

3. What do I do if my family objects, does not understand my calling, or disbelieves?

– Be patient; give them time. Or you may have to accept that they may never fully understand your call.

– Teach them about ministry through personal example.

– Engage the prayers of your spouse and immediate family for your ministry.

– Keep in mind that your ministry may be the reason the unsaved members of your family come to Christ.

4. What about my inadequacies or shortcomings?

– Know that the effectiveness of your ministry is not determined by you, but by the anointing God has placed within you.

5. How will opportunities to minister be made available to me?

– If God has given the gift, He will make room for it.

– As long as there are those in need there will be opportunities to minister. In Matthew 9:37 (NIV), Jesus said, *"The harvest is plentiful but the workers are few."* Serve where you are needed.

6. How can I overcome my reluctance to commit to God's call?

– Know that you will have to answer to God.

– Know that you will not fulfill your purpose.

THE CALL TO COMMITMENT

7. What will happen if I don't obey God?

– Many souls may be lost, left comfortless, or discouraged.

– God will not be pleased. Does this bother you?

8. How do I overcome my fears of speaking publicly?

– Fear should not be a deterrent to ministry. It is a natural emotion to have whenever you are faced with uncertainty. David said to put your trust in God; *"What time I am afraid, I will trust in thee"* (Psalm 56:3, KJV).

9. Why me? Why not someone else?

– Only God knows the answer to that question.

10. I've been told I don't "look" like a minister. What can I do to fit into the traditional stereotype of what a minister should "look" like or be?

– Don't try to fit into someone else's view—be yourself!

"...the LORD said to Samuel, 'Do not consider his appearance or his height, for I have rejected him. The LORD does not look at the things man looks at. Man looks at the outward appearance, but the LORD looks at the heart'" (1 Samuel 16:7, NIV).

11. How important is licensing or ordination?

– Neither affects effectiveness.

– Prepare yourself through study and commitment.

THE CALL TO COMMITMENT

- If becoming licensed or having credentials is your goal, find out what is required in your church or denomination and pursue it. The bottom line is don't stop ministering.

12. How should I select a good Bible school?

- Check with schools within your denomination. Evangelical-based colleges or seminaries are likely good choices.

- Visit college websites, review catalogs, and ask questions of others who have attended similar institutes of higher learning.

13. My past life was less than stellar. Will those who knew me before I was saved and committed to ministry accept me now?

- No one is perfect. All saints are reformed sinners. In your ministry, you will have the responsibility and the opportunity to share the saving grace of our Lord just as Saul did when he converted and became Paul. It may take a while for others to accept your new found calling, but remain faithful.

14. Until now ministry service has not been one of my interests. Is this just a phase?

- Only God can answer that question. Seek His face for your answer. Maybe ministry is a second career for you; or it may be a phase. Seek God for your answer.

THE CALL TO COMMITMENT

DISCIPLINES REQUIRED TO BECOME AN EFFECTIVE MINISTER

Discipline: a conduct or pattern of behavior that when performed according to standards, results in growth and improvement of a skill.

Disciplines necessary for ministers:

1. Submission
2. Accountability
3. Study
4. Prayer
5. Worship
6. Self-control
7. Service
8. Love

The next pages will help you reflect on cultivating and growing the disciplines required of ministerial service. You will reflect on your strengths and weaknesses in these areas and set goals for yourself. Keep in mind that no one is perfect and that includes ministers! Prayer and diligence are required to achieve the level of discipline required by your spiritual commitment.

THE CALL TO COMMITMENT

SUBMISSION

Definition: to retire, withdraw. The condition of being humble, or compliant. Accepting authority or control from another.

Key Scripture
Submitting yourselves one to another in the fear of God. (Ephesians 5:21)

Your favorite scripture concerning "submission"?

_____
_____
_____

Reflection: your personal standards and goals regarding "submission"?

_____
_____
_____
_____
_____
_____
_____

THE CALL TO COMMITMENT

ACCOUNTABILITY

Definition: an obligation or willingness to accept responsibility for one's behavior; the ability to explain or qualify actions.

Key Scripture

And it came to pass, but when he was returned, having received the kingdom, then he commanded the servants to be called unto him, to whom he had given the money, that he might know how much every man had gained by trading. (Luke 19:15)

Your favorite scripture concerning "accountability"?

_____
_____
_____

Reflection: your personal standards and goals regarding "accountability"?

_____
_____
_____
_____
_____
_____

THE CALL TO COMMITMENT

STUDY

Definition: to give attention and diligence, especially with the intention of learning.

Key Scripture
Study to show thyself approved unto God, a workman that needeth not to be ashamed, rightly dividing the word of truth. (2 Timothy 2:15)

Your favorite scripture concerning "study"?

_____
_____
_____

Reflection: your personal standards and goals regarding "study"?

_____
_____
_____
_____
_____
_____
_____

THE CALL TO COMMITMENT

PRAYER

Definition: communication with God in earnest word or thought.

Key Scripture

And he spake a parable unto them to this end, that men ought always to pray, and not to faint. (Luke 18:1)

Watch ye therefore, and pray always, that ye may be accounted worthy to escape all these things that shall come to pass, and to stand before the Son of man. (Luke 21:36)

Your favorite scripture concerning "prayer"?

_____
_____
_____

Reflection: your personal standards and goals regarding "prayer"?

_____
_____
_____
_____
_____
_____

THE CALL TO COMMITMENT

WORSHIP

Definition: to show extravagant respect or admiration for; reverence offered a divine being.

Key Scripture
Give unto the Lord the glory due unto his name. Bring an offering, and come before him; worship the Lord in the beauty of holiness. (1 Chronicles 16:29)

Your favorite scripture concerning "worship"?
_____
_____
_____

Reflection: your personal standards and goals regarding "worship"?
_____
_____
_____
_____
_____
_____

THE CALL TO COMMITMENT

SELF-CONTROL

Definition: the act of restraining one's behavior related to impulses, emotions, or desires.

Key Scripture
But I keep under my body, and bring it into subjection: lest that by any means, when I have preached to others, I myself should be a castaway. (1 Corinthians 9:27)

Your favorite scripture concerning "self-control"?
_____
_____
_____

Reflection: your personal standards and goals regarding "self-control"?
_____
_____
_____
_____
_____
_____

THE CALL TO COMMITMENT

SERVICE

Definition: work done to benefit others; actions that contribute to the welfare of others.

Key Scripture

For we are laborers together with God; ye are God's husbandry, ye are God's building. (1 Corinthians 3:9)

Your favorite scripture concerning "service"?

_____
_____
_____

Reflection: your personal standards and goals regarding "service"?

_____
_____
_____
_____
_____
_____

THE CALL TO COMMITMENT

LOVE

Definition: strong affection, attachment, and devotion towards another; the attitude of God towards his Son and mankind.

Key Scripture

And now these three remain: faith, hope, and love. But the greatest of these is love.
(1 Corinthians 13:13)

Your favorite scripture concerning "love"?

_____
_____
_____

Reflection: your personal standards and goals regarding "love"?

_____
_____
_____
_____
_____
_____

THE CALL TO COMMITMENT

QUESTIONNAIRE FOR MINISTERS SEEKING CREDENTIALS

Most ministers want to obtain the legal and professional credentials from their church and denomination. In my denomination, ministers are ordained through a process involving local and state organizations. Since this process varies greatly among Christian groups, it is wise to consult senior church leaders before beginning this journey. But at some point, regardless of your denomination, you will be asked to respond in writing or during an interview to questions regarding your ministerial calling and objectives. The following list is a few general questions typically asked of all candidates for credentials.

THE CALL TO COMMITMENT

Questionnaire for Ministers Seeking Credentials

Name: _____

How do you wish to be contacted?

Phone: _____   Text: _____

Email: _____

Mail: _____
       ADDRESS

       _____
       CITY   STATE   ZIP

Please answer the following questions as honestly and thoughtfully as possible using additional paper if necessary. Your answers will help the pastorate guide you towards your interests, and determine appropriate service during your preparation for credentials track time.

1. When did you first feel you were called to ministry? Explain.

   _____
   _____
   _____
   _____

2. What was your initial reaction to your calling? Describe.

   _____
   _____
   _____

THE CALL TO COMMITMENT

3. Who did you first share this information with? Spouse, friend, pastor, other? What was their reaction?

_____
_____
_____
_____

4. To what area of ministry are you called? Why? Be specific. Do you feel this area of ministry requires ordination to perform? Why?

_____
_____
_____
_____

5. How many years have you been actively involved in ministry? What did you do, where did you do it, how long did you do it, with what age group, etc.?

_____
_____
_____
_____

6. What have you learned from ministry to make you confident that you are a good candidate for Credentials?

_____
_____
_____
_____

THE CALL TO COMMITMENT

7. Concerning your ministry, what do you feel are your gifts and/or talents? Why?

   _____
   _____
   _____
   _____

8. What is the highest level of education you completed? What are your plans for future education?

   _____
   _____
   _____
   _____

9. List any other formal or informal religious training in which you participated. Include the dates and names of the sponsoring organizations.

   _____
   _____
   _____
   _____

Part Three:
Understanding the Worship Experience

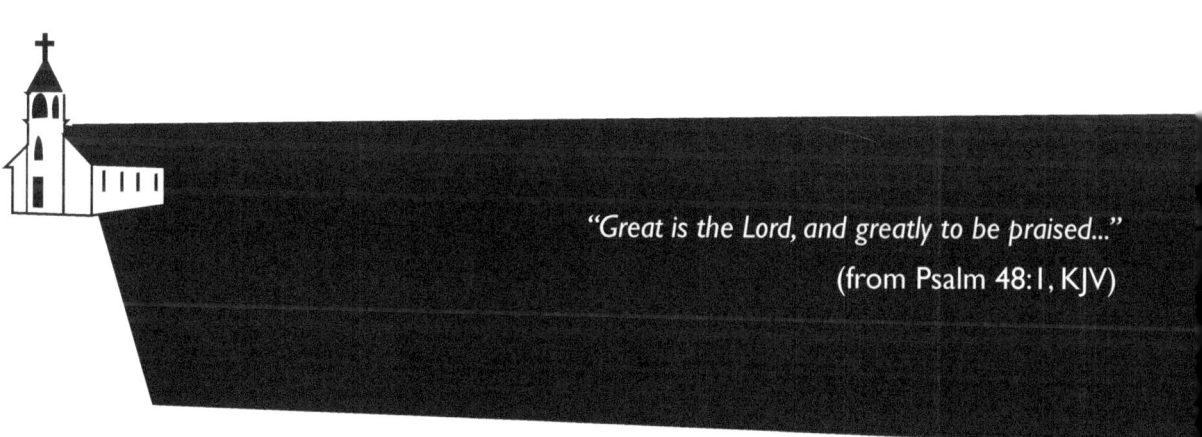

"*Great is the Lord, and greatly to be praised...*"
(from Psalm 48:1, KJV)

TRUE WORSHIPPERS, WORSHIP TRULY

"Yet a time is coming and has now come when the true worshipers will worship the Father in spirit and truth, for they are the kind of worshipers the Father seeks. God is spirit, and his worshipers must worship in spirit and in truth."

(John 4:23–24, NIV)

UNDERSTANDING THE WORSHIP EXPERIENCE

UNDERSTANDING WORSHIP

A minister's personal relationship with God is enhanced through the worship experience. If the minister understands worship, he or she will be able to lead the church in a meaningful worship experience.

The graphic below depicts what ministers need to understand about worship:

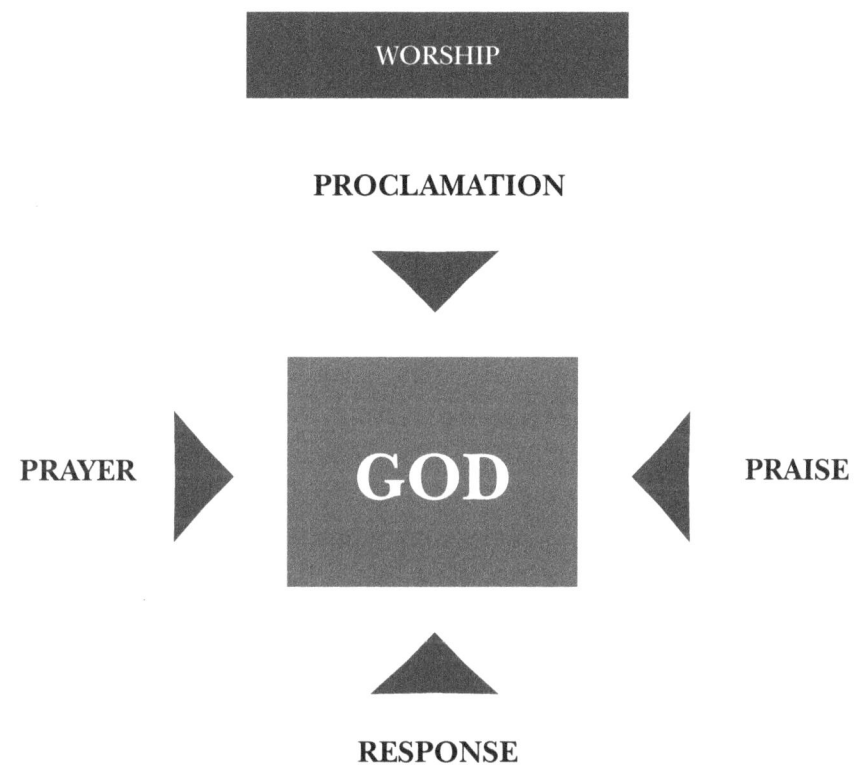

God must be the center of our worship.

God is the center of every aspect of the worship experience.

Essentially there are four parts to every worship service.

> **Praise** is an expression of approval or admiration, of gratitude and devotion for blessings received. Praise is the acknowledging of God's perfection, works, and benefits.
>
> *PRAISE GOD for who He is, was, and will be.*

UNDERSTANDING THE WORSHIP EXPERIENCE

Prayer is supplication or intercessory prayer for another. It is the expression of our dependence on God.

PRAY TO GOD as the One who gives and sustains life.

Proclamation (or preaching) is the delivery of a text based upon Scripture, the inspired Word of God.

PROCLAIM GOD as Savior and Lord.

Response is the appropriate action taken when one receives an answer from God.

RESPOND TO GOD with conviction and affirmation.

We Worship God Because [of]...

What God Is Doing in the Present

Each day that we are alive is a manifestation of God's ability to create and maintain all that He has created. The fact that we are alive with a beating heart is cause to worship. The birth of a baby, the replenishing of plant and animal life, as well as the continuation of the earth itself is more than enough reason to worship God.

What God Has Done in the Past

The Bible is filled with historical events that speak to what God has done in the past. These historical events play a huge part in allowing man to understand the kinds of acts God is capable of. As we read about the God of Abraham, Isaac, and Jacob, we must recognize that God is the source behind the unfolding drama contained in biblical history. More importantly to worship, however, is the fact that when we remember our past and reflect on God's goodness and mercy, we worship Him because of what He has brought us through.

UNDERSTANDING THE WORSHIP EXPERIENCE

Moses, when remembering God's strength and power, praised God by saying:

> *"I will sing unto the Lord, for he hath triumphed gloriously: the horse and the rider hath he thrown into the sea. The Lord is my strength and song, and he is become my salvation: he is my God..."* (from Exodus 15:1–2, KJV).

Moses knew that by himself he was no match for Pharaoh. So, God gave him the victory over Pharaoh. He led the Children of Israel through the Red Sea, and he led the people in a worship experience.

What God Will Do in the Future

When we remember how God sustains His creation(s), and all the things He has done in your life, it is these experiences that give us reason to worship God.

HOW DOES ONE WORSHIP?

Real worship is a spiritual undertaking. Jesus said, *"God is a Spirit, and they that worship Him must worship Him in Spirit and in truth"* (John 4:24, KJV). Thus, spiritual worship is the type of worship that connects to the soul. Spiritual worship implies that there is a sense of God's presence that is felt internally. There is the realization that God and His worshippers are on one accord. While clapping or raising hands and stomping feet both play a part in the worship experience, they are only instruments that enhance the worship experience.

To worship in the Spirit means to have focus—meaning that a person who is worshipping in spirit knows why he or she is doing so—it is not an unconscious act. While worshipping in spirit may manifest itself through an emotional outburst, it may also be reflected in stillness. It was David who said, *"Make a joyful noise,"* and who also said, *"Be still and know...."* And, it was *"beside the still waters"* that David was restored.

Worship allows for a cleansing of the soul to take place. As one comes into the presence of God and hears the message of God, like Isaiah, he or she will see their imperfections.

> *"Then said I, Woe is me! For I am undone; because I am a man of unclean lips...for mine eyes have seen the King, the LORD of hosts"* (Isaiah 6:5, KJV).

UNDERSTANDING THE WORSHIP EXPERIENCE

Our human nature leads us to seek something or someone to worship. It is a natural act. The worship experience serves to satisfy man's quest for God. If the true God is not known or is denied, we will out of necessity worship a substitute or a false god.

GOD, THE OBJECT OF WORSHIP

The worship service is a celebration in honor of God based on who God is and what God does. The celebration is enhanced as worshippers are reminded of what God is presently doing in their lives, what God has done in the past, and what (by faith) God will do in the future.

> *"Make a joyful noise unto the LORD, all ye lands.*
>
> *Serve the LORD with gladness:*
>
> *come before his presence with singing.*
>
> *Know ye that the LORD he is God;*
>
> *it is he that hath made us, and not we ourselves;*
>
> *we are his people, and the sheep of his pasture.*
>
> *Enter into his gates with thanksgiving,*
>
> *and into his courts with praise:*
>
> *be thankful unto him, and bless his name.*
>
> *For the LORD is good: his mercy is everlasting;*
>
> *and his truth endureth to all generations"*
>
> (Psalm 100, KJV).

In the above psalm, Israel is summoned to praise the Lord. Of whom is the psalmist speaking?

UNDERSTANDING THE WORSHIP EXPERIENCE

God as Creator

The revelation of God as Creator unfolds in the Bible's opening statement: "In the beginning God..." a statement which clearly announces that with God was the beginning of all created things.

All of creation testifies to the fact of God as Creator. The delicate snowflake, the endlessly moving waterfall, the translucent wings of a butterfly, the tiny ant on his way home with tomorrow's meal, a sunset, a sunrise, all defy the wisdom of humanity; no part of creation can be duplicated except by the Creator.

God as Sustainer

"See how the lilies of the field grow" (from Matthew 6:28, NIV).

God cares for His creation. Therefore, not only is He the Creator of all things, but He sustains all things He creates.

God Revealed Through Jesus Christ

Many who answer the call of ministry have asked to be shown God, to which Jesus responds in John 14:9, *"Anyone who has seen me has seen the Father."* Thus, through Jesus who went about doing good, meeting the needs of the sick and needy, and performing miracles, we see God. The very person of God and the nature of God are revealed through the acts of Jesus, His Son.

The fact remains that no amount of logic or reason is adequate to define God. Only through personal experience with Jesus, the Son, can we truly know who God is.

PART FOUR:
Understanding Corporate Worship

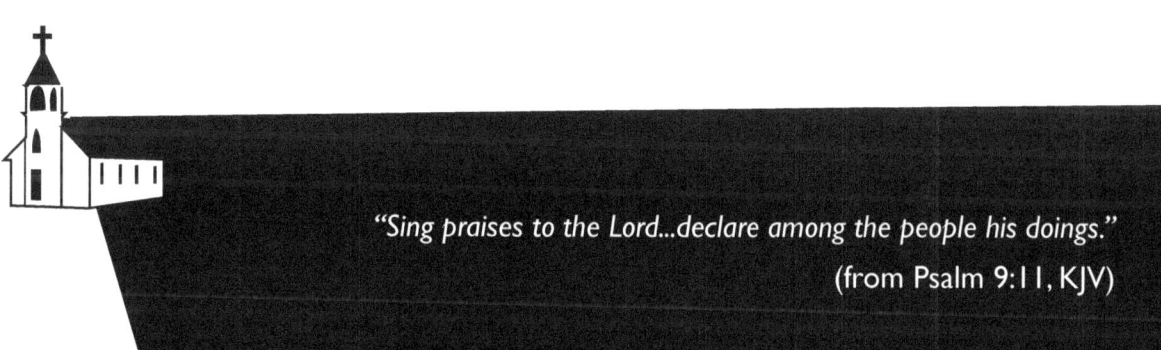

"*Sing praises to the Lord...declare among the people his doings.*"
(from Psalm 9:11, KJV)

THE CALL TO WORSHIP

"Praise the LORD. Praise God in His Sanctuary; praise Him in His mighty heavens. Praise Him for His acts of power; praise Him for His surpassing greatness. Praise Him with the sounding of the trumpet, praise Him with the harp and lyre, praise Him with tambourine and dancing, praise Him with the strings and flute, praise Him with the clash of cymbals, praise Him with resounding cymbals. Let everything that has breath praise the LORD. Praise the LORD."

(Psalm 150, NIV)

UNDERSTANDING CORPORATE WORSHIP

LEADING THE CHURCH IN WORSHIP

"They who minister to the church at worship serve effectively only when…each act is done out of a sense of mission and with a spirit challenged by the meaning behind it" (paraphrased—Rev. James E. Massey).

Praise God in His Sanctuary! Corporate worship (the coming together of the people of God) rejuvenates and renews. In Psalm 73, the psalmist was unable to understand the prosperity of the wicked, until he went into the sanctuary to worship. Then he understood. In the 100th Psalm we are encouraged to willingly and joyfully worship and praise before the Lord…

"Make a joyful noise unto the LORD, all ye lands.

Serve the LORD with gladness: come before his presence with singing.

Know ye that the LORD he is God: it is he that hath made us and not we ourselves:

we are his people, and the sheep of his pasture.

Enter into his gates with thanksgiving, and into his courts with praise:

be thankful unto him, and bless his name.

For the LORD is good; his mercy is everlasting;

and his truth endureth to all generations"

(Psalm 100, KJV).

Among the many responsibilities required of ministers is that of leading the church in worship. The flow of a worship service differs from church to church based on the particular traditions and/or preferences of the church. The various segments of a worship service, while done differently, are basically the same and serve the same purpose—to worship and glorify God.

This section is intended to give leaders an overview of the steps necessary to lead a worship service regardless of various traditions or preferences. The goal is to encourage leaders to think about ways to unify and improve upon the service and to make worship a meaningful experience for all who participate.

Understanding Corporate Worship

Worship service, when properly guided, provides an opportunity for the congregation to experience the power and the presence of God. Those in leadership should strive to keep the worship experience on track by:

- Being on time
- Being prepared
- Being focused
- Being alert

Be on Time

For anyone leading a worship service, timeliness is critical. Timeliness honors the presence of God and your commitment to the church that service will begin on time.

One should plan to arrive at least 30 minutes prior to the beginning of the service. During that time it is suggested that one prepares for the service by engaging in prayer—alone or with others who will be assisting in the worship experience. Then, at the set time, the leader should be in place ready to begin the worship service.

Be Prepared

The readiness of the worship leader(s) greatly affects the tone of the worship service.

> *"These people come near to me with their mouth and honor me with their lips, but their hearts are far from me. Their worship of me is made up only of rules taught by men"* (from Isaiah 29:13, NIV).

- Preparation begins with prayer before you get to church.
- Preparation requires readiness in heart and spirit, which is accomplished only through prayer.

- Preparation means that you come with help, Bible, songbook, etc.

With additional help the Holy Spirit will assist you in leading the congregation into worship decently and in order, in spirit and in truth.

Be Focused

Understand and know what worship means and lead accordingly. Through their leadership abilities, the worship leader helps the congregation experience the power and the presence of God. This experience, if left unmet, could leave worshippers wanting in their worship experience.

Be Alert

It is important that worship leaders give directions that help to smoothly transition the worship service from one segment to the next. Basic instructions/directions like "please stand" or "you may be seated" may seem unimportant, but if directions are not given at appropriate times during the service it could lead to confusion (especially if there are visitors in the sanctuary). For example, if songbooks or hymnals are used, the page number or title of the song should be announced if the congregation is expected to participate. If the congregational song is not in the songbook, the leader should prompt the congregation with a call and response format to allow them to follow along with the words of the song.

Remember, the person who leads the church in worship must actually guide the congregants through the process. Do not leave the service to chance where people are wondering what to do next.

UNDERSTANDING THE SEGMENTS OF THE WORSHIP SERVICE

Here, the term *segment* refers to the various parts of the worship service that when combined make up the *order of service*. The order in which the segments are presented is not the same in all churches.

Call to Worship

This is an appeal to congregants to enter in and worship. The purpose of which is to call the church "to order." The call may take the form of a prayer, a Scripture reading, or a simple summons. It is the first order of business conducted in the worship service. A greeting or brief comments relative to the worship experience may be given, thus preparing the congregation for participatory worship.

Invocation

The invocation is a prayer that honors and invites the presence of God into the worship service. Typically, it is the prayer that starts the worship service. The prayer need not be too long; it can be a prayer given by the minister or it can be read directly from Scripture. In some churches, the Call to Worship and the Invocation are the same.

General Prayer

Sometimes referred to as the Pastoral Prayer, this prayer lifts the concerns of the church. The person who is asked to perform this prayer ought to be attuned to the needs of the congregation. If you are unsure of how to start this prayer, it does not hurt to let the Holy Spirit guide your words.

Reading of Scripture

All services should include the reading of God's Word. The reading may be done responsively (with audience participation) or by one reader. Whenever possible, the Scripture selection should relate to the overall theme of the service.

Sacred Music

Music includes the choir, congregation, soloists, groups, or instruments. A variety of song types should be selected, including praise songs, songs of affirmation, salvation, and hope.

Church Announcements

It is through the church announcements that congregants are called to serve. Attention should be given to preparing the announcements so that members will be made aware of the church's events and happenings, which, in fact, are opportunities and requests for service. Verbal announcements are significant because people tend to pay attention to and remember what they hear as well as what they read.

Welcoming of Visitors

There should always be an acknowledgment and welcome given to visitors to join the congregation in worship.

Tithes and Offering(s)

The giving of tithes and offerings is biblically based. To do so represents obedience and thanksgiving to God.

Understanding Corporate Worship

Offertory Prayer

This is a prayer of thanksgiving and dedication of tithes and offerings. This, too, does not need to be a long prayer. First Chronicles 29:11–13 is one of my favorites.

Meditation

This is the time to listen and hear from God. It is a time for reflection and contemplation.

Sermon Prelude Prayer

The minister acknowledges the need for God's anointing prior to starting the message. Often the pastor will offer this prayer himself or herself, but other times they may ask someone else to offer the prayer.

Sermon

The proclamation of God's Word is the apex of the worship service.

Invitation to Discipleship

The invitation to accept Christ or join the church offers an opportunity for individuals to reflect and respond to the total worship experience. It may be followed by conviction, contrition, acceptance of Jesus Christ, and even personal praise and thanksgiving.

Altar Prayer

The altar prayer is designed to lift up any special needs or concerns of the church before the Lord. It may be done by the pastor or someone else he or she has designated.

Benediction

A benediction is a prayer for God's blessings upon the people at the end of the worship service. Sometimes it includes thanksgiving for God's presence during the service or a request for God's protection until the next time the congregation gathers together.

The benediction was practiced in the Old Testament (see Numbers 6:22–27) as well as in the New Testament (Luke 24:50). The biblical gesture for imparting the benediction is usually outstretched arms with palms extended over the congregation while the congregation stands with bowed heads.

Every segment of the worship service, from the Call to Worship to the Benediction, should reverence God in spirit and in truth.

UNDERSTANDING CORPORATE WORSHIP

REFLECTIONS

1. Write a Call to Worship, using Psalm 34:3 as your opening statement.

_____
_____
_____
_____
_____
_____
_____

2. From the Bible, read the prayers below. How might the contents be used in a corporate worship experience?

John 17

_____

1 Chronicles 29:10b

_____

1 Chronicles 29:13–14

_____

Exodus 15:1–19

_____

Jude 24–25

_____

Psalm 19:14

_____

Understanding Corporate Worship

3. Consider Jesus' teachings in Matthew 6:9–13 regarding prayer. Using the principles of praise, penances, and petition, compose a general prayer suitable for corporate worship.

_____

_____

_____

_____

_____

_____

4. Compose a brief prayer for each of the following segments of the worship service:

Altar prayer

_____

_____

_____

_____

_____

_____

Benediction

_____

_____

_____

_____

_____

Understanding Corporate Worship

Invocation

_____
_____
_____
_____
_____
_____

Offertory prayer

_____
_____
_____
_____
_____
_____

Sermon prelude

_____
_____
_____
_____
_____
_____

Understanding Corporate Worship

5. Check your understanding of the worship segments to the total worship experience by indicating the area of worship (praise, prayer, proclamation, response) in which the following segments fall:

Call to worship   _____

Invocation   _____

General prayer   _____

Reading of Scripture   _____

Sacred music   _____

Church announcements   _____

Welcome to visitors   _____

Tithes and offerings   _____

Offertory prayer   _____

Sermon prelude prayer   _____

Sermon   _____

Invitation to discipleship   _____

Response   _____

Altar prayer   _____

Benediction   _____

> *"They who minister to the church at worship serve effectively only when each act is done out of a sense of mission and with a spirit challenged by the meaning behind it."* —James E. Massey (paraphrased)

GLOSSARY OF TERMS FOR LEADING THE WORSHIP SERVICE

Amen: *It is so; so be it; assent*

Corporate Worship: *The act of celebrating God in a group setting*

Devotion: *A short religious service combining prayer, reading of Scripture, or comments relative to worship*

Hallelujah: *(Heb.) Praise ye Jehovah*

Praise: *Commendation, expressed approval of God*

Prayer: *Supplication, intercession, petition directed to God*

Proclamation: *An announcement or declaration (preaching, teaching)*

Response: *The decision or action following the proclamation of the Word of God*

Segments of worship: *The various parts of the worship service which, when combined, make up the total order of the service*

Worship: *The act of celebrating God for who God is, what God has done, and what, by faith, we know God will do; the heart's expression of praise and adoration to God*

Understanding Corporate Worship

Suggested Bible passages for leading the congregation into various segments of worship.

Call to Worship
Lamentations 3:22–24
Psalm 150
Psalm 100
Isaiah 12:2 5–6
Habakkuk 2:20
Psalm 33:1–3
Revelations 19:5–7

Call to Prayer
Hebrews 4:15–16
Psalm 55:16–17, 22
Psalm 62:5
Proverbs 3:5–6

Benediction
Jude 24–25
Revelation 22:21
2 Corinthians 13:14

Call to Stewardship
Deuteronomy 16:16
Exodus 15:2
Malachi 3:8–10

Questions for the Worship Leader

1. What is worship? What is the worship leader trying to lead or help people to do?

_____

_____

_____

_____

Answer: Worship is the act of celebrating and honoring God for who He is, what He has done, what He is doing, and what He will do.

Understanding Corporate Worship

2. What is the difference between corporate worship and private worship?

_____

_____

_____

_____

Answer: Corporate worship involves an audience. Private worship is for the individual.

3. Why is it necessary for someone to lead the church in worship?

_____

_____

_____

Answer: To assure proper thought, sequence, timing; to give the service structure; to prevent chaos; to assure order.

4. What kind of preparation does the worship leader need before serving?

_____

_____

_____

Answer: To be spiritually attuned and knowledgeable regarding the order of service.

UNDERSTANDING CORPORATE WORSHIP

5. Who are the people who attend our worship service?

_____

_____

_____

Answer: Members, visitors, seekers, saints, unbelievers, curious

6. How might knowing who our worshippers are affect our presentation?

_____

_____

_____

Answer: It helps to keep us focused.

UNDERSTANDING CORPORATE WORSHIP

THE CALL TO CORPORATE PRAISE

The Psalmist says:

"Praise him with the sounding of the trumpet,

praise him with the harp and lyre,

praise him with tambourine and dancing,

praise him with the strings and flute,

praise him with the clash of cymbals,

praise him with resounding cymbals.

Let everything that has breath praise the LORD"

(from Psalm 150:3–6, NIV).

The call to praise is found many times in the Bible. It is a summons to the people to express appreciation, or to say "thank you" for the person and/or provisions of God.

Real and expressed praise forces one to acknowledge God for who He is and what He does because of His love, His goodness, and His mercy.

Who God Is

GOD IS LOVE.

God sent His Son to save us—the ultimate expression of love.

GOD IS GOOD.

He sent the sunshine and the rain, the harvest, and the grain to assure sustenance for our physical bodies.

UNDERSTANDING CORPORATE WORSHIP

GOD IS MERCIFUL.

When we exceed His boundaries and go after other gods, He has mercy and gives us another chance.

The psalmist does not set out to define God. He summons Israel to praise God based on the "fact" of God: the God of Israel; Jehovah; the *"I Am That I Am"* of Moses, Abraham, Isaac, and Jacob. Polytheism (having more than one god) was not allowed in Israel. Only the one God was acceptable, and the psalmist assumed as much in his summons to worship:

"Praise the Lord.

Praise (honor) God in his sanctuary;

(Israel's sacred place of worship)

(Our place of worship)

praise Him in his mighty heavens (sun, moon, stars).

Praise Him for His acts of power (what He does);

Praise Him for his surpassing greatness.

...Let everything that hath breath praise the LORD"

(Psalm 150:1–2, 6, NIV).

(The psalmist infers that one should remember what God has done in creation, in the world, and in your life.)

The nation of Israel experienced bondage under the hands of the Egyptians for more than 400 years. The suffering had at times been unbearable. God (the God of Israel, Abraham, Isaac, and Jacob) had been their deliverance through the hands of Moses. They were just beyond the Red Sea when Moses led the nation in praise:

Understanding Corporate Worship

> *"I will sing unto the Lord, for he hath triumphed gloriously: the horse and his rider hath he thrown into the sea. The Lord is my strength and song, and he is become my salvation: he is my God..."* (from Exodus 15:1–2, KJV).

A little later, Miriam the prophetess, and sister of Moses, took a timbrel in her hand and led all of the women in praise and dance. Miriam summoned them to praise: *"Sing to the Lord, for he hath triumphed gloriously..."*

Who am I? Why do I need to praise?

Humans have a need to worship that includes praise born out of grateful hearts. There is a vast difference between man and God. Moses said, *"The Lord is my strength."* He knew that by himself, he was no match for Pharaoh. Likewise, the nation on its own was no match for Egypt. It was the Lord who was due the praise!

The nature of man and woman leads them to seek something or someone to worship. It is a natural act. If the true God is not known or is denied, we will, of necessity, worship a false god.

Praise disallows complaining. A grateful heart is a happy heart. It recognizes blessings and does not wallow in misfortunes.

Praise rejuvenates and renews as one reflects on reasons to be thankful.

THE CALL TO CORPORATE PRAYER

Because prayer is a key element in the worship service it is important that the person leading the prayer be an effective prayer leader.

Prayer has been defined as intercession, supplication, petition to God. It includes praise, petition, and penance.

Prayer is a key element in the worship service. While some churches rely on formal liturgical traditions, many do not. This section is devised to help the person leading the public prayer to develop suitable prayers. Keep in mind that it is important that the person who performs the prayer understands the purpose of the prayer and how to fulfill that purpose in prayer.

1. Use inclusive terminology. For example, you might say:

> "Dear God, *we* thank You...."

> "Bless *us* with Your presence today...."

> "You are *our* Savior...."

One's personal needs should not dominate the prayer. However, if there is a need to make a prayer personal, in special cases or emergency needs, the transition back to the audience should be made as quickly as possible.

There are at least three basic parts to any prayer:

A. Prayers of Adoration and Praise—includes addressing God (examples: Father, God, Lord, Dear God, Heavenly Father, etc.) and expressions of love, affirmation, adoration (thank You, for Your blessing of salvation, etc.).

B. Prayers of Petition—includes requests for all needs (i.e., physical, emotional, spiritual, economic).

C. Prayers of Penance—asks for forgiveness for all wrongs, both known and unknown.

UNDERSTANDING CORPORATE WORSHIP

REFLECTIONS

Some call Matthew 6:9–13 the "model prayer." While this prayer may serve as a model, it is not the only prayer which one may pray. Let's examine it to identify the three parts mentioned (praise, penance, and petition).

Our Father which art in heaven	_____
Hallowed be thy name	_____
Thy kingdom come,	_____
Thy will be done on earth,	_____
as it is in heaven.	_____
Give us this day our daily bread.	_____
And forgive us our debts,	_____
as we forgive our debtors.	_____
And lead us not	_____
into temptation,	_____
but deliver us from evil.	_____
For thine is the kingdom,	_____
and the power,	_____
and the glory, forever.	_____
Amen.	_____

Note that the prayer begins by addressing God as "Our Father." The first petitions relate to God and His plan and program. The other petitions relate to our needs. The prayer is concluded with a doxology, a liturgical interpolation from 1 Chronicles 29:11.

Understanding Corporate Worship

There are many types of prayers used in the corporate setting. The minister should comply with the requested type of prayer. The most common prayers fall into the following categories. Let's review:

Invocation

Honors and invites the presence of God into the worship service. Usually brief and to the point. Sometimes serves as the Call to Worship, as part of the Call to Worship, or following the Call to Worship.

General Prayer

Lifts the concerns of the church. The person who is asked to perform this prayer ought to be attuned to the needs of the congregation.

Offertory Prayer

Expresses thanksgiving and dedication of tithes and offerings.

Sermon Prelude Prayer

Acknowledges the need for God's anointing prior to delivering the message.

Altar Prayer

Lifts up any special needs or concerns of the church before the Lord.

Benediction

Asks for God's blessings upon the people at the end of the worship service.

THE CALL TO CORPORATE PROCLAMATION

The proclamation of the Word is the core of the worship experience. Praise and prayer provide opportunity for the people to speak to God. The proclamation should be a time when God speaks to the people. The person who has the awesome responsibility of speaking for God needs to be one to whom and through whom God can speak.

The "proclaimed" word needs to be:

Inspired

No study or preparation can take the place of inspiration. Inspiration stimulates man under divine control to deliver the truth as given from God.

The Bible is the inspired Word of God. Its meaning and interpretation at a given time, under different circumstances, needs to be inspired by the Holy Spirit in order to meet the needs of the people.

Informational

Second Timothy 2:15 (KJV) says, *"Study to shew thyself approved unto God, a workman that needeth not to be ashamed, rightly dividing the word of truth."* The message needs to have content. This requires study and preparation. The Holy Spirit will bring to one's memory only that which has been studied.

Relevant

The message must meet the needs of the people where they are in order for the message to be meaningful.

Communicated

For these purposes, communicate means to impart thoughts, ideas, information, by speaking. The messenger, the message, and the receiver are all involved in the process. The minister is the messenger, the message should be the anointed Word of God, and the receiver is the audience. The messenger should speak to the people in a way that can be understood. Simplicity of language and words spoken clearly are keys to the art of good communication.

Note: This lesson is not intended to be an instructional piece for sermon preparation, only to the extent that it will cause the preacher or teacher to think about the awesomeness of the task. While the author does not consider herself to be an authority on preaching, she has made observations which will be shared.

THE CALL TO CORPORATE RESPONSE (THE ALTAR)

The opportunity for response to the proclamation takes place in different ways and in different places of the church, depending upon custom, tradition, or in a given church or denomination. Some congregations take respondents to what is called "the prayer room." Others use the altar. This section, while dealing specifically with the altar as the place for response, could also be a guide for churches that do not use the altar method.

It is not uncommon that ministers or persons are appointed or trained for this very important part of the worship experience.

The worship experience is incomplete without the moment of decision which often centers at or around the altar. This chapter is devoted to understanding the altar and its purpose as the culminating factor in the worship experience. It is further intended to be a help for those who minister to the respondents at the altar.

It is understood that churches handle persons responding to the message (proclamation) differently. The methods used at the public altar, the prayer room, or other designated places are different, depending upon the denomination or the church. However, while the methods are different, those who come are responding to the information received during the proclamation or other aspects of the service which have taken place. Some may even come because of personal evangelism or other forms of outreach which the church members may have been involved in prior to the service.

The people who come to the altar usually do so for one of three reasons:

(1) To become new converts to Christ,

(2) To renew their commitment to Christ, or;

(3) To receive prayer for special concerns.

While all aspects of the worship service are instrumental in bringing one to the altar, it is usually the sermon (proclamation) which brings someone to the point of conviction, decision–making, or emancipation.

The altar worker assists the respondent in these areas by counseling (helping them to think through the information received), praying for them, and helping them to act upon the information by making a decision for Christ.

The following pages are intended to help the minister understand the altar's meaning and purpose.

UNDERSTANDING CORPORATE WORSHIP

THE ALTAR: A PLACE OF WORSHIP

"What then shall we say, brothers? When you come together, everyone has a hymn, or a word of instruction, a revelation, a tongue or an interpretation. All of these must be done for the strengthening of the church" (1 Corinthians 14:26, NIV).

Worship: *act of celebrating and honoring God for who He is and what He has done.*

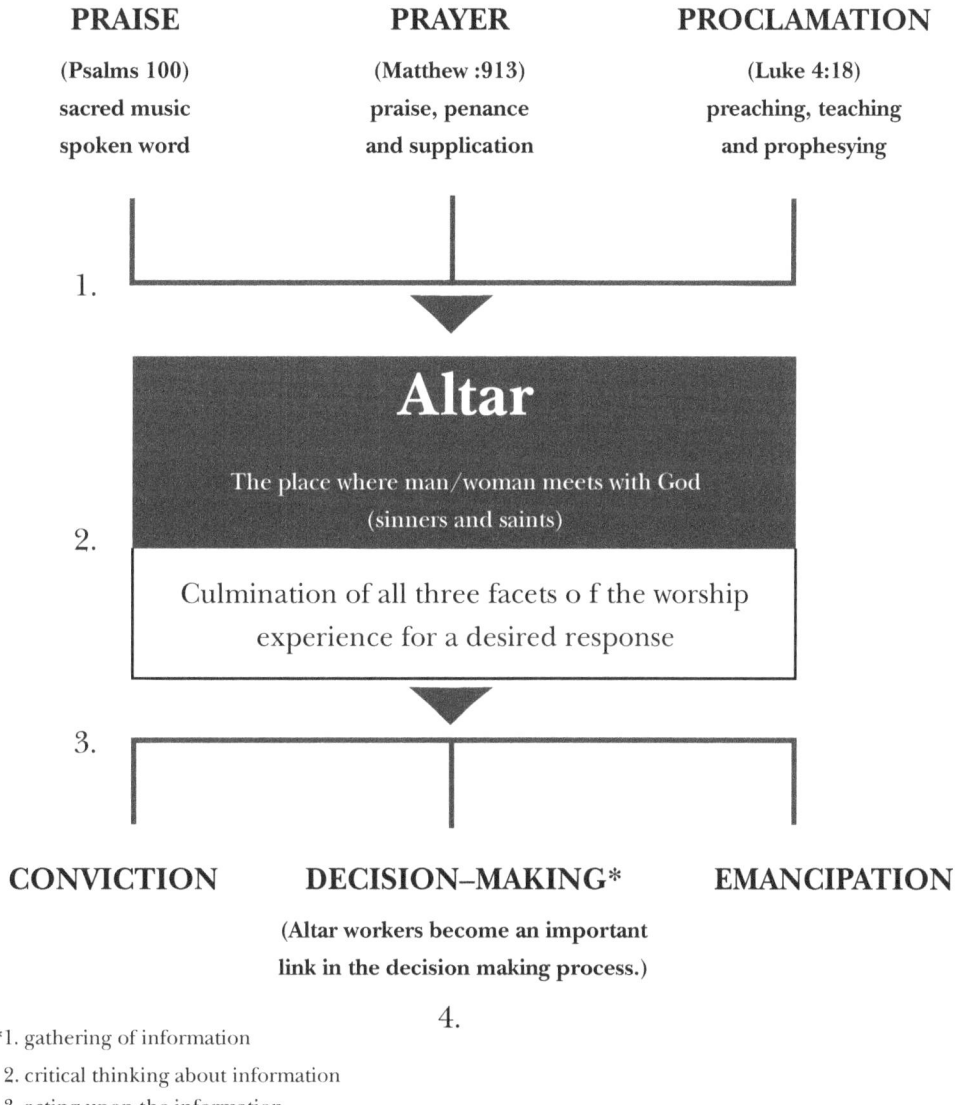

PRAISE
(Psalms 100)
sacred music
spoken word

PRAYER
(Matthew :913)
praise, penance
and supplication

PROCLAMATION
(Luke 4:18)
preaching, teaching
and prophesying

1.

Altar

The place where man/woman meets with God
(sinners and saints)

2.

Culmination of all three facets o f the worship experience for a desired response

3.

CONVICTION   **DECISION–MAKING***   **EMANCIPATION**

(Altar workers become an important
link in the decision making process.)

4.

*1. gathering of information
2. critical thinking about information
3. acting upon the information

Note: Look at the following pages for chart analysis.

Understanding Corporate Worship

A study of the chart on the previous page reveals the significance of the altar in its relationship to the worship experience. Also to be noted is the role that the altar worker plays in assisting in the decision-making process which is often a part of the altar experience.

(1) PRAISE, PRAYER and PROCLAMATION lead to the time of REPONSE which may take place at the (2) ALTAR, or other designated place depending on the custom of the church. Whatever the custom, when the invitation to accept Christ is given, this becomes an important part of the service. (3) As all other facets of the worship experience have been realized, CONVICTION, DECISION-MAKING, and EMANCIPATION of the seeker become the desired conclusion. The (4) ALTAR WORKER is an important link in this whole process.

Conviction

The point at which the sinner realizes and acknowledges that he or she is a sinner. Conviction is the result of the work of the Holy Spirit in the hearts of the sinner. It is the first step to repentance. *"God have mercy on me, a sinner"* (from Luke 18:13, NIV).

Decision-Making

At no point in the worship service is decision-making more prevalent than at altar time. It is the result of the gathering of information and critical thinking about the information which leads to action (i.e., acceptance of Jesus Christ as Savior and Lord).

Emancipation

Freedom from sin and its consequences through the atonement of Christ. *"For it is by grace you have been saved, through faith—and this not from yourselves, it is the gift of God"* (Ephesians 2:8, NIV). The acceptance of salvation can take place anywhere, but the altar has played an important role in being the point of contact for the seeker.

THE ALTAR: ITS MEANING AND PURPOSE

"And Noah builded an altar unto the LORD; and took of every clean beast, and of every clean fowl, and offered burnt offerings on the altar.

And the LORD smelled a sweet savour; and the LORD said in his heart, I will not again curse the ground any more for man's sake" (Genesis 8:20–21, KJV).

The Old Testament

In Patriarchal times, holy places were places where it had proven to be possible to meet with God. Such places were marked with an altar and sacrifice.

    A. A place of sacrifice

        The sacrifice was made by the shedding of blood of unblemished animals for the removal of sin and guilt (Exodus 29:36).

    B. A place to meet with God

        – Jacob at Bethel (Genesis 35:1)

        – Gideon (Judges 6:19–24)

        – Manoah (Judges 13:19–20)

    C. A place designating an event in which man had had an encounter with God

        – Abraham at Sichem (Genesis 12:6–7)

        – Abraham at Bethel (Genesis 12:8)

    D. In the tabernacle

        – The altar of incense (Exodus 30:1–6)

        – Symbolic of Christ our Intercessor through whom our prayers and praise ascend to God (John 17:1–16; Hebrews 7:25)

        – The altar of burnt offering

        – The altar on which animals without blemish were sacrificed for the sins of the people (Leviticus 1:3–4)

The New Testament

The altar is based on the fact of the atonement, the body of Christ broken for the remission of sins (Hebrews 10:5; 1 Corinthians 11:23–27).

– As a place of prayer (Hebrews 4:16)

– As a place of sacrifice (Romans 12:1)

The Altar Worker/Minister: Priest

The Bible has much to say about persons who pray for the people, presenting their needs and concerns at the altar. The minister will do well to study this section thoroughly because of the role which he or she will play in this regard as a part of ministry. All ministers will have the responsibility and opportunity to pray for people, either at the altar or in other situations, and help to lead them in making decisions about accepting salvation. The word "minister" and "priest" are used interchangeably in this chapter, as the minister is also called to priestly function.

Ministers/Priest: Called to this Position

"And no man taketh this honour unto himself, but he that is called of God, as was Aaron" (Hebrews 5:4, KJV).

"Another thing to remember is that no one can be a high priest just because he wants to be. He has to be called by God for this work in the same way God chose Aaron" (Hebrews 5:4, NIV).

Elements of Priesthood

Normally we think of a priest as one who intercedes for the people. Moses gives the idea of Old Testament priesthood as consisting of three elements (Numbers 16:5):

condition—to be chosen or set apart for Jehovah as His own

qualification—to be holy

function—to be allowed to come to, or to bring near Jehovah

Understanding Corporate Worship

Priestly Function

Moses said to Aaron, *"Come to the altar and sacrifice your sin offering and your burnt offering and make atonement for yourself and the people; sacrifice the offering that is for the people and make atonement for them, as the LORD has commanded"* (Leviticus 9:7, NIV).

Agents in Altar Outcomes

The minister who meets with the seeker at the location of the altar for the purpose of praying with and for them serves as an agent in:
- decision-making
- conviction
- emancipation
- other needs

Requirements of the Priest

1. Knowledgeable of the Word of God

Often the answers to questions raised at the altar can be found in Scripture.

"Do your best to present yourself to God as one approved, a workman who does not need to be ashamed and who correctly handles the word of truth" (2 Timothy 2:15, NIV).

2. Filled with the Holy Spirit

"For the Holy Spirit will teach you at that time what you should say" (Luke 12:12, NIV).

"This is what we speak, not in words taught us by human wisdom but in words taught by the Spirit, expressing spiritual truths in spiritual words" (1 Corinthians 2:13, NIV).

3. Filled with Wisdom

"The fruit of the righteous is a tree of life; and he who wins souls is wise" (Proverbs 11:30, NIV).

UNDERSTANDING CORPORATE WORSHIP

REQUIREMENTS OF THE PRIESTHOOD (MINISTRY)

Read the following passages of Scripture from both the Old Testament (figurative) and the New Testament (actual).

Figurative (Leviticus 8:6–12)	**Actual**
1. Cleansed (v. 6)	2 Timothy 2:21
2. Clothed (v. 7)	Ephesians 6:14–17
3. Crowned (v. 9)	Ephesians 6:14–17
4. Anointed (v. 10)	1 Samuel 16:13

Write your interpretations from the New Testament passages below as it relates to the minister who is an altar worker.

1. _____

2. _____

3. _____

4. _____

ALTAR METHODOLOGY

Altar methodologies will vary from church to church depending on a number of factors, including culture, denomination, and tradition. The following suggested methodology will provide guidelines only for churches which follow a formal altar call, allowing individuals to come to the altar for prayer. It is intended to offer guidelines, not to replace whatever method is used for your church.

The altar prayer is the culmination of the worship experience. The altar worker assists the hearer with encouragement and prayer to respond to what has already taken place. Comments and prayers are most helpful when they relate to the sermon and enforce its theme.

    1. Pray for God's guidance

        – Approach an altar candidate with a smile, a friendly gesture.

    2. To a kneeling candidate

        – Kneel beside him or her (if possible).

        – If the seeker is already praying, the altar worker should also pray silently momentarily before interrupting.

    3. Body contacts

        – Grasp a hand.

        – Put an arm around one's shoulder.

        – Avoid an embrace unless you know it is OK (especially members of the opposite sex).

    4. Lead–in lines

        – My name is...

        – May I pray with you? / Would you like me to pray with you? / May I help? / Is there something special that you'd like me to pray about?

        – May I ask...what is your name?

5. Preparing to pray

- Listen attentively to what the seeker is saying.

- Note: Is the person seeking salvation (note page 95 for help in leading a person to Christ)? Is this a reaffirmation of one's faith? Are there special needs or burdens?

- Be sure that you understand the need, then indicate what you will be praying for, summarizing or articulating the need.

6. Praying with or for the altar person

- Address the needs that are at hand.

- Pray softly. The prayer is between you, the person for whom you are praying, and God.

7. Wrap it up

- Do not place pressure on someone to make a commitment.

- If a commitment to Christ is made, this needs to be expressed publicly to be celebrated by the congregation. Remain with the person until this has been done.

- If the person is shy or unwilling to speak publicly, you may speak for them, giving the content of their testimony.

- Introduce the person by giving their name and the fact of their commitment.

- The minister will introduce the person to the church and give further directions.

- If one does not make a commitment to Christ, allow them to return to their seat quietly. Assure them of your continued interest and prayers for their problem or concern which they may have shared with you.

UNDERSTANDING CORPORATE WORSHIP

THE USE OF SCRIPTURE IN ALTAR WORK

"The entrance of thy words giveth light; it giveth understanding to the simple" (Psalm 119:130, KJV).

Faith Passages

- Psalm 37:5

- Psalm 56:3

- Matthew 21:22

- 2 Corinthians 5:7

Prayer Passages

- Philippians 4:6

- Hebrews 4:16

- 1 John 5:14

Salvation passages in the book of Romans make the explanation simple.

- Romans 3:23—the fact of sin

- Romans 3:10—none are righteous

- Romans 5:12—Adam's seed corrupt

- Romans 5:6, 8—Christ died for the ungodly (us)

- Romans 6:23—the penalty of sin

- Romans 10:13—Call on the Lord to be saved

- Romans 10:9–10—Confess Christ and believe

Other significant passages are:

- John 3:16—the gift of salvation

- John 5:24; John 6:44–47—assurance of eternal life

- Psalm 51:5—born in sin

DOS AND DON'TS FOR ALTAR WORKERS

– Do be conscious of personal hygiene (breath and body).

– Do not divulge altar secrets shared by the seeker.

– Do not give counsel at the altar except when leading one to Christ (especially regarding marriage problems) because of the complexity of the situation and the fact that the information is one-sided.

– Do keep your promise to continue to pray for that person.

Prerequisites for Altar Workers

– Born-again Christian

– Compassionate

– Trustworthy

– Knowledge of "altar work" Scripture

– Concern for lost souls

– Knowledge on how to intercede for others in prayer

– Able to communicate

– Sensitive to the leading of the Holy Spirit

– Desire for the salvation of souls

Checklist for would-be altar workers

( ) Have you considered the importance of this task?

( ) Have you prayed for divine wisdom and guidance?

( ) Have you given thought to the best approach for helping a seeker at the altar?

( ) Are you willing to help the seeker find Christ, and are you willing to help follow-up with this new convert?

Understanding Corporate Worship

( ) Have you engaged in fasting and sincere prayer for God to use you in this special work?

( ) Do you believe God has called you to altar ministry?

Review the Minister's Affirmation found in Part 1 as you proceed to serve in Altar Work.

PLEDGE

I believe that God wants me to serve as an altar worker because...

_____
_____

therefore, *(write what you will do to improve your service as an altar worker)*

I pledge to...

_____
_____
_____

UNDERSTANDING CORPORATE WORSHIP

REFLECTIONS

Write your definitions of the following words and phrases as they relate to altar work. Use your Bible dictionary or dictionary of the English language to help you if necessary.

Born-again Christian: _____
_____

Compassionate: _____
_____

Trustworthy: _____
_____

Knowledgeable of altar work Scriptures: _____
_____

Concern for lost souls: _____
_____

Knowledgeable about interceding for others: _____
_____

Able to communicate: _____
_____

Sensitive to the leading of the Holy Spirit: _____
_____

ALTAR WORKERS TRAINING

Most churches have a specific protocol for conducting altar calls. This is to ensure uniformity and coordination in the way altar workers perform their duties. This section explains what altar workers do and will help you create a step-by-step guide for personal reference.

1. ## What is the purpose of the Altar Call?

   At my church: this is an invitation extended from the pulpit to members of the congregation to come forward and become new converts, renew spiritual commitment, and receive collective prayer.

   At your church? _____
   _____
   _____
   _____

2. ## Why do people come to the altar for prayer?

   At my church: salvation or spiritual needs, family or personal matters, healing or deliverance.

   At your church? _____
   _____
   _____

3. ## Who works at the altar?

   At my church: ministers, deacons, and other appointed prayer intercessors.

   At your church? _____
   _____

Understanding Corporate Worship

4. What is expected of an altar worker?

At my church: To follow and support the pulpit prayer and not compete with it or other altar workers nearby. To quietly pray with and for individuals who respond to the altar call.

At your church? _____

_____

_____

_____

5. Preparing to serve during the Altar Call

At my church: altar workers are asked to prepare on three levels; 1.) naturally (proper hygiene and attire, breath mints, etc.), 2.) mentally (create in me a clean heart, O God and a right spirit within me, Psalms 51:10), and 3.) spiritually by invoking guidance and assistance from the Holy Spirit.

At your church? _____

_____

_____

_____

6. What to do when the Altar Call appeal is made from the pulpit?

At my church: some ministers come to the front of the church and face the congregation. Others position themselves behind the responders. In some instances, the pulpit leader may direct an altar worker to a specific responder or location.

At your church? _____

_____

_____

UNDERSTANDING CORPORATE WORSHIP

7. What should be avoided during the Altar Call?

At my church:

A. Embracing or hugging responders unless invited to do so. Women typically pray with women and men with men.

B. Repeating any concerns overheard from praying responders or otherwise violating altar confidentiality.

At your church? _____

_____
_____
_____
_____

8. What is the role of altar workers when the prayer ends?

At my church: If a responder expressed a desire to be a new convert or member, the altar worker remains with them and introduces them to the congregation when prompted by the pulpit leader. Everyone else returns to their seats.

At your church? _____

_____
_____
_____
_____

A SERVICE OF CELEBRATION—
THE LORD'S SUPPER

It is now time for us to participate in reliving the moment during which these words were spoken by our Lord. We do so as an act of obedience and as a memorial to our Lord's death by crucifixion.

> **(The minister will move to the podium and will pause as the deacons and ministers (those serving communion) take their places at the communion table.)**

The setting in which these words were spoken was somber. Our Lord's time had come. He would soon (in a matter of hours) be:

> *"But he was piered for our transgressions, he was crushed for our iniquities; the punishment that brought us peace was upon him, and by his wounds we are healed"* (Isaiah 53:5, NIV).

The crucifixion of Jesus was necessary because He was the only acceptable sacrifice. He alone could atone for our sins. He chose to do "the will of the Father" to bring the world back into a right relationship with God.

Before participating in this service, we are cautioned by the apostle Paul thusly:

> *"Wherefore whosoever shall eat this bread, and drink this cup of the Lord, unworthily, shall be guilty of the body and blood of the Lord. But let a man examine himself, and so let him eat of that bread, and drink of that cup. For he that eateth and drinketh unworthily, eateth and drinketh damnation to himself, not discerning the Lord's body"* (1 Corinthians 11:27–29, KJV).

Understanding Corporate Worship

Only the FORGIVEN one is worthy to partake of this communion. The forgiven one is not one who has not sinned, but it is one who...

> *"That if you confess with your mouth, 'Jesus is Lord,' and believe in your heart that God raised him from the dead, you will be saved"* (Romans 10:9, NIV).

(Let us pray.)

Dear God, may all who sit in this audience today examine himself in light of the cross, and in discernment of the Lord's Body, be worthy to partake of this bread and cup. We pray that today, all will ask for and accept forgiveness for past sins, and receive Jesus as Lord and Savior. In the name of Jesus, Amen.

> *As the cups are passed by our deacons and ministers, I ask that all will sit quietly reflecting upon the meaning of this service. We will wait until all have been served. We will then commune together.*

(The cups will be passed by deacons and ministers.)
(At this point, appropriate music will be played.)

When all have been served, the minister will say:

> *"This cup of blessings of which we bless; is it not the communion of the blood of Christ?"*

Understanding Corporate Worship

The minister will raise the bread and say:

> "The Lord Jesus the same night in which He was betrayed, took bread: And when He had given thanks, He brake it, and said, Take, eat, this is my body which is broken for you. This do ye in remembrance of me" (1 Corinthians 11:23, NIV).

The minister will say:

> **"Let us eat together."**

> "After the same manner also He took the cup, when He had supped, saying, This cup is the new testament in my blood: this do ye, as oft as ye drink it, in remembrance of me" (1 Corinthians 11:24–25, KJV).

The minister will raise the cup and say:

> **"Let us drink together."**

> "For as often as ye eat this brean and drink this cup, ye do show the Lord's death till he comes" (1 Corinthians 11:24–25, KJV).

Jesus concluded the supper with these words:

> "But I say unto you, I will not drink henceforth of this fruit of the vine, until that day when I drink it new with you in my Father's kingdom" (Matthew 26:29, KJV).

Let us never forget. Let us conclude this service, not only remembering His death and suffering, but also looking forward to His promised return.

(Please hold your cups until they have been properly collected.)
(Appropriate music—including congregational—will conclude the communion service.)

Part Five:
The Ministry at Work

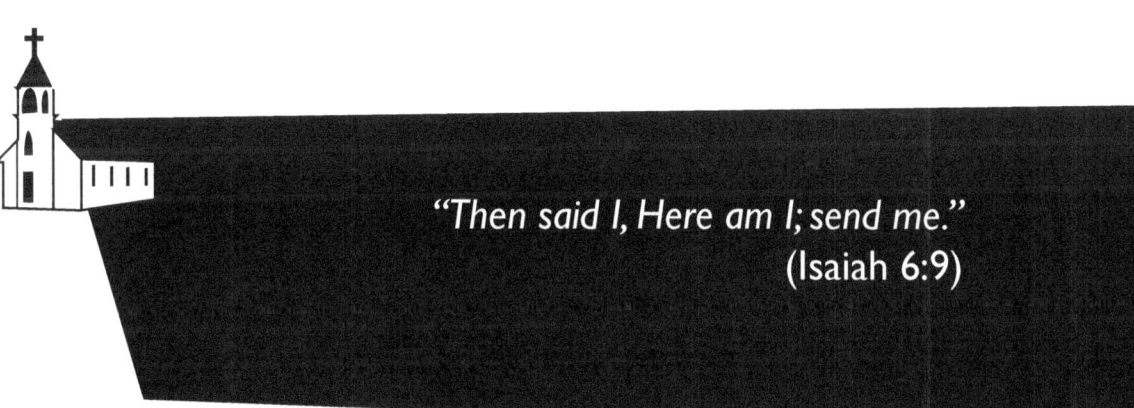

"Then said I, Here am I; send me."
(Isaiah 6:9)

THE MINISTRY AT WORK

DOS AND DON'TS WHEN VISITING THE SICK

All ministers will visit the sick or shut-ins in the hospital, nursing home, or private home at some time or other. It has been mandated in Scripture. The following dos and don'ts are intended to serve as a guide, especially for ministers-in-training. However, there are exceptions to all rules. When in doubt, the minister in training should pray for God's guidance or consult with another more experienced minister.

DOS

Do pray beforehand in order to prepare yourself spiritually and mentally to face the sick person or the family.

Do be aware of hospital administrative requirements, visiting hours, and procedures.

Do pay attention to "isolation" or "no visiting" signs and respect them. If the door is closed, make sure it is OK to enter the patient's room.

Do have some knowledge of the patient's condition before you visit. Find out if the visit is acceptable or desired. Get this information from the family (preferably) or the doctor.

Do keep in mind the physician is in charge of the sickroom. Whatever you do, do in conjunction with the physician's requests and requirements. Excuse yourself when the doctor comes in unless he or she asks or permits you to stay.

Do pay attention to mechanical apparatus. Be careful of where you sit or stand; sitting on the bed may jar the patient, causing discomfort.

Do excuse yourself when the patient's meal is being served; unless it is asked that you stay or it is necessary for you to assist the patient in eating.

Do excuse yourself when other visitors or family members are present unless you are asked to remain.

THE MINISTRY AT WORK

Do be mindful of your body language. Pity, fear, judgment, and love are all expressed through your body language; be careful not to send the wrong message.

Do use safety precautions. Wear gloves or masks when suggested by hospital or family. Wash your hands with soap and water or hand sanitizer upon leaving the bed side of a sick person. Also, don't use the patient's private washroom.

Do be a good listener. The patient or family member(s) may need to talk about their concerns and fears. Do not downplay the reality of their physical or mental pain.

Do make your visits short. Make it a rule to complete your visit in a timely manner. Offer to pray with the patient (or family), read Scripture or any other appropriate ministerial function, and then leave.

Do seize the opportunity to minister to the soul. Minister to the patient as well as the family about the saving grace of our Lord.

Do keep all conversations confidential. Remember, it is not your place to discuss the medical condition of someone you are ministering to, even if it is with the patient's family.

DON'TS

Don't engage in controversial subjects or conversation. Words have power. Let your words be encouraging and meaningful.

Don't be judgmental. This is not the time to make disparaging comments or engage in negative thinking; this right is reserved for God.

Don't give unsolicited advice regarding treatment. As a minister, your opinion is probably highly valued in these types of situations. However, remember, you are not a doctor. Encourage the patient and family to be mindful of the doctor's recommendations.

The Ministry At Work

Don't be a prophet of doom. A sick person doesn't need to be reminded of the seriousness of their illness, nor does he or she need to be compared to another person with the same type of illness. Limit your personal opinions/stories to ones of encouragement.

Don't pretend to be God's spokesperson by basing your information on generalities or "old wives' tales."

Don't make promises of healing unless you are certain of God's will. Encourage the patient to have faith in God, and let them know that you also have faith in God for their healing.

Don't discuss the patient's condition with others in the room, even if the patient appears comatose.

THE MINISTRY AT WORK

WHAT MUST I DO TO BE SAVED?
(Leading Someone to Christ)

Every minister of Jesus Christ wants to hear someone ask, "What must I do to be saved?" This section is intended to help make answering that question easier by summarizing the Plan of Salvation. Whether new converts are won at the altar, in the prayer room, or simply one on one outside the four walls of the church, the questions and responses will be pretty much the same in all instances. It is a good idea to memorize as much of the following information as possible, or carry a copy of this information with you to enable you to answer questions about salvation clearly and succinctly.

WHAT MUST I DO TO BE SAVED?

Believe on the Lord Jesus Christ (Acts 16:31)

– Believe that God loves you and wants to save you.

– Believe that Jesus died to save you and that He has paid the price for your sins.

WHEN CAN I BE SAVED?

Now!

– "Now is the time of God's favor; now is the day of salvation" (from 2 Corinthians 6:2).

HOW CAN I BE SAVED?

By accepting Jesus as Lord and Savior

– Accept Him by faith (John 20:29).

– Accept Him as Savior; He died for your sins (Matthew 20:28).

– Accept Jesus as Lord; He is the one you will love, worship, and obey (Luke 6:46).

The Ministry At Work

By repenting of your sins

– Admit you have sinned (Romans 3:23).

– Commit to turn away from sin.

By praying

– Ask to be forgiven by God.

– Ask God to save you.

– Thank God for forgiving and saving you.

By acknowledging Jesus as Lord and Savior (Romans 10:9)

– Tell others that He is your Savior and Lord. This includes family and friends.

Sample prayer

Dear God, thank You for sending Jesus to die for me on the cross that I might be saved. Please forgive me for all my sins and save me. Cleanse me from any future sins. I accept You as my Lord and Savior. Thank You. Amen.

The minster should:

– Pray for the enabling power of the Holy Spirit to lead a person to Christ.

– Believe that God wants to save the seeker. Your faith lays the groundwork for the Holy Spirit to lead you in this task.

– Speak to the core of God's plan for salvation, explaining each point as you move along. An opportunity to teach about how to live a Christian life will come later.

THE MINISTRY AT WORK

The minister should tell the seeker:

–He or she may know they are saved because God said it.

"God so loved the world, that He gave his only begotten Son, that whosoever believeth in him should not perish, but have everlasting life" (John 3:16, KJV).

– We are saved by grace (God's goodness) (Ephesians 2:8–9).

– God's grace is everlasting (Lamentations 3:22, 23; Psalm 23:6).

THE MINISTRY AT WORK

THE GRAVESITE CEREMONY

The gravesite ceremony usually follows the funeral service, either held at the church or at the funeral home. In some cases families have opted to make the gravesite service the only service.

The following procedures, though variable, can help to give dignity to the service.

1. The minister walks in front of the casket, leading the procession to the gravesite. (Optional: reads appropriate Scripture while walking)

2. The minister takes his or her position at the head of the casket. (The pallbearers or funeral director will advise regarding the head of the casket.) The minister should wait for the casket to be placed on the burial site and until the procession (especially the family) is in place.

3. The service begins with the minister speaking to the family. The minister will give brief remarks: words of comfort and encouragement, for the family and words of appreciation for friends who are at the gravesite. Because the service is outside, remarks should be brief and to the point.

4. The minister prays.

    – An acceptable prayer might be the Lord's Prayer from Matthew 6:9–13 (KJV recommended); the minister may pray in his or her own words or pray the following:

    Dear God,

    A dear loved one has been taken from us. We are thankful for all of the memories that will keep (name of deceased) alive in our hearts. We are grateful that you have allowed (him/her) to be an important part of our lives. We pray for this family that you will soften the blow of death with the certainty of Your abiding presence. Give them the strength to face today and the future minus a loved one.

    For now, ease the pain. And when they have suffered enough, take away the pain. Give strength for today, bright hope for tomorrow.

    Dear God, because You are a loving God, we commit each family member and loved one to You. Amen.

THE MINISTRY AT WORK

5. The committal:

The minister reads appropriate committal service Scripture and makes comments regarding the committal (lowering of the casket) of the body.

The minister may use his or her own words, or may choose to use the following:

As we prepare now to return the body of our loved one to its kindred dust, we know that we leave [his/her] spirit with God. And our God, the Righteous Judge, will do what is right. Knowing that there is a time appointed for all living to die, let those of us who are left face the challenge to do what is right, and let us put our trust in Him who said, "I am the resurrection and the life. He who believes in me will live, even though he dies, and whoever lives and believes in me will never die" (from John 11:25, NIV).

Next, the minister repeats the following or similar words as flower petals are strewn on the casket:

Forasmuch as it has pleased Almighty God, in his wise providence to take out of this world the soul of our deceased brother/sister/friend, we therefore commit [his/her] body to the ground, earth to earth, ashes to ashes, dust to dust, looking for the general resurrection in the last day and the life of the world to come, through our Lord Jesus Christ.

The minister gives the final prayer of benediction.

SUGGESTED HELPS

The minister may select as many or as few appropriate passages as necessary for the service.

Comfort: Psalm 23; 27:1–5, 14; 90:1–12; John 5:24–29; 11:25–26; 14:1–6; Job 19:25–27

Benediction: 2 Corinthians 13:14; Jude 24–25; Philippians 4:23

THE MINISTRY AT WORK

HOUSE CALLS TO THE BEREAVED

Pray

Before you visit, ask for God's guidance in making your visit a blessing. Each family you visit will have their own unique needs.

Call

Call the family to make sure that the family wishes to be visited before you go. If the time is inappropriate, work with the family's schedule to find out if there is a better time for the visit.

Meet and Greet

Meet and greet all family members and friends present. Introduce yourself to those family members or friends who may not know you. Long titles are unnecessary and usually not impressive. It is probably best to give your title as it relates to the church that you represent. Some may not be members of your church. You will want to make an effort to speak to everyone present.

Express Condolences

For example, "The church was very sorry to hear of your loss. We have been praying that God's presence will surround you and your family during this time."

Wait and Listen

The family may need to express their grief. Don't ask too many questions regarding the cause or circumstances of the death. Allow the family to tell you what they want you to know.

Ask questions and offer assistance

Ask what the church can do to help during this time of bereavement. If this is not the time to discuss funeral arrangements, find out when it would be appropriate to have such a discussion. Ask if the family will accept prayer. If they do, pray for the situation that is at hand. You may want to preface the prayer with an appropriate reading of Scripture and use that passage as the basis for your brief comments.

Be Discreet

Do not place blame or pass judgment regarding the decreased or family members.

Keep Your Visit Brief

During the time of bereavement, the family need not be bogged down with meaningless visits and conversation. So, strive to keep your visit meaningful and short.

THE MINISTRY AT WORK

BIBLICAL FOUNDATIONS OF MARRIAGE

Love and relationships pose issues of importance to church members. Ministers are often asked to talk to engaged couples prior to marriage, participate in marriage ceremonies, or work with married couples. This section provides three documents to help start what will undoubtedly become an archive of materials to assist you in this area.

COMPONENTS

1. A Scriptural Basis for Marriage.

2. 10 Questions for Couples Prior to Marriage

3. Tips for Keeping a Christian Marriage Alive: "Just Stay There" is a presentation given at my church. "Ask Reverend Dise" is a collection of excerpts from a weekly online column that I once authored.

These materials help create a framework and make it easier for new ministers to discuss relationships with parishioners. However individuals who appear to have mental or emotional needs that require more than discussion should be advised to seek professional help.

THE MINISTRY AT WORK

A SCRIPTURAL BASIS FOR MARRIAGE

Marriage (Genesis 2:18, 23, 24)

Marriage was created because of the need for:
   v.18 — companionship
   v.18 — a helper

Man's companion, taken from his side, would have:
   v.23 — kinship/commonality

Maintenance of the union would require:
   v.24 — commitment
   v.24 — oneness/unity

Which other scriptures are relevant to your view of marriage?

_____
_____
_____
_____
_____

Which other scriptures are important to the tenets of your church doctrine regarding marriage? _____

_____
_____
_____
_____

THE MINISTRY AT WORK

10 QUESTIONS FOR COUPLES PRIOR TO MARRIAGE

It is a common practice for ministers to discuss important issues with couples prior to performing a wedding for them. This list of questions will help the couple focus on biblical principles to form a strong foundation upon which to build their marriage.

1. What scriptures have you selected to build your marriage relationship?
2. How would you like to have feelings of love and respect shown to you?
3. In what ways do you need to improve communication between the two of you?
4. In what ways are you different from one another? How are you similar?
5. What are the strengths you possess as a couple?
6. Is there anything that annoys you or makes you angry with your fiancé?
7. How will you resolve differences and conflicts?
8. Have you discussed family issues such as children?
9. How will you maintain intimacy and keep your marriage alive?
10. In addition to praying and attending church together, in which other Christian activities will you participate to help keep your marriage strong?

OUR COMMITMENT TO MAKING OUR MARRIAGE LAST

We _____ and _____
      (SIGNATURE, PERSON 1)   (SIGNATURE, PERSON 2)

discussed these questions with _____
                                        (MINISTER'S SIGNATURE)

on this date _____

We pledge with God's help, we are committed to making our marriage endure.

THE MINISTRY AT WORK

STAY THERE!
(How to Stay There)

This essay is my answer to that often asked question, "Sister Dise, what do you mean when you say "stay there"? This statement has long been associated with my comment to the question, "how do you stay with someone for so long"? I usually say, "just stay there". My husband and I celebrated our 71st wedding anniversary in 2019. I cannot address all the issues that might be involved in a marriage relationship, but I will try to give some basics for maintaining a marriage.

First, let me define for this setting, my definition of a marriage. I do not want to be guilty of suggesting that all who live together, even with legal backing, have a marriage. Let it be understood that I am talking about the relationship in which the basic components of marriage are present.

> The book of Matthew records the word of Jesus regarding marriage:
>
> *"have you not read, that he which made them at the beginning made them male and female. And said, for this cause shall a man leave father and mother, and shall cleave to his wife, and they twain shall be one flesh; wherefore they are no more twain, but one flesh. What God hath joined together, let not man put asunder* (Matthew 19:4-6 KJV)

I believe that a marriage is a union of a male and a female. The relationship is one in which no other person (family or friend) is allowed to come between the two. The couple is united in purpose, though not agreeable at all times as to how the purpose will be attained. The relationship requires that both work at the permanence of the marriage. They are bound by a God-given bond that exists between the two. I will now discuss 10 points to help strengthen this bond and make "staying there" a reality.

1. **Remember your vows.** There was a commitment made between you, your mate, and … God.

The Ministry At Work

2. **Keep focused.** What were your goals in the first place? Ask yourself, why did I marry this person? What do/did I really want? Do not lose your focus because of trivial things.

3. **Appreciate your mate for their uniqueness.** Do not try to make them like someone else, or like somebody else's mate. You do not have to impress anyone with your choice. Learn how to live with whom you married.

4. **Benefit from your differences.** The "one flesh" does not mean that you give up your identity or that your mate gives up their identity. The fact that you view things differently can be an asset. The marriage can have twice as many benefits.

5. **Communicate.** Talk and listen with your heart as well as the ear. Discuss not only what was said, but what was meant. If you are uncertain of one's meaning, keep talking and listening. Sometimes, the second time around makes for a clearer understanding.

6. **Do not hold anger.** The Bible urges us to "not let the sun go down on our wrath". (Ephesians 4:26). This is especially important in a marriage. Forgive means to grant pardon; to cease resentment against a person for an act committed against you. Get over it!

7. **Solve the problem.** Let everything you say or do be for the purpose of solving the problem, not for placing blame, getting even, out doing, or out talking the other person. Avoid emotionally charged statements intended as personal attacks. Wounds are difficult to heal so try hard not to make them. Practice self-control. Take a walk. Calm down. Wait until you are ready to come to the bargaining table.

8. **Work together.** Be each other's best buddies. Appreciate each other's contributions. Tell your mate how you thank him or her for their contribution.

9. **Play together.** The Bible says a "merry heart maketh a cheerful countenance". (Proverbs 15:13). Laugh with each other. Do not be too busy to break the rou-

THE MINISTRY AT WORK

tine of work. Balance work and play. It's okay to play games with your mate. It's lawful. It's expedient. It's helpful in the relationship. Find the time to enjoy each other. Do it often.

10. **Pray together.** In her books, Christian author Elizabeth Elliot describes the marriage relationship as a triangle, with God at the top and the husband and wife at the opposite corners. The closer you get to God, the closer you are to each other. I concur with Elliot. When all else fails, let the both of you pray to "stay there".

THE MINISTRY AT WORK

ASK REVEREND DISE

Dear Rev. Dise:

We have been married for 10 years. We love each other, but over the last six months or so, we've grown apart. We go to church and try to pretend that everything is fine so that no one can sense our problems. But we really don't communicate at home, and get into more heated discussions than ever. When people ask you to share the secret of a successful marriage, you've often say "stay there". How do you stay there if you are unhappy? Doesn't God want us to be happy?

      Signed,

         Unhappy

Dear Unhappy:

Let me begin by saying that the phrase "stay there" explains how a couple manages to add years to their marriage, but this is not the only secret to a happy union. Communication is basic to a successful marriage because it is the only way concerns, feelings, and intentions of the partner can be known. It requires listening as well as speaking to the issues with the intent of both persons getting an understanding. Do you know the reasons for each other's unhappiness? You say you don't communicate. Plan a time to talk together about what you have told me. It may well be that's all needed.

The Ministry At Work

Dear Rev. Dise:

I have been living with my boyfriend for seven years now and I just recently became a new Christian. I still care a lot for him and I know that it's not right to live with somebody who is not my husband, but the lease on the apartment we are in won't be up until next year. Is it wrong for me to stay with him until then? What should I do? I am a single mother and I really can't afford to live by myself. Do you have any suggestions?

        Signed,
           Trapped

Dear Trapped:

You mentioned living with your boyfriend for seven years, but there is no mention of plans to marry, now or later. You say you care a lot for him. Does he feel the same way about you? Or is the relationship, as you seem to infer, just a convenient situation for the both of you? The Bible says, "marriage is honorable in all, and the bed undefiled". (Hebrews 13:4) If you love each other and you wish to live together, why not get married? If you don't care for each other, the whole situation is one of deception.

The Ministry At Work

Dear Rev. Dise:

Please pray for me and my husband. We attend separate churches and he has stopped attending his church. He doesn't want to go to my church. I found out he has been seeing another woman. I want to leave him and get a divorce. He says he is sorry and he will start attending church and he will never see the woman again. I don't trust him. I want to seek counseling, but he refuses to go. I love my husband but don't know what to do. Please keep us in prayer.

    Signed,

        In Prayer

Dear In Prayer:

Adultery destroys trust, a very important component of a marriage. Without trust, it becomes very difficult to keep a marriage together. However I note that in your closing statement, you indicate that you still love your husband and that he says he is sorry. I assume you believe him. It seems to me that though you have been hurt, there is a possibility for healing. I suggest that before you make a move to dissolve the marriage, that you seek God for guidance. Divorce is not always the easiest way out of a dilemma.

THE MINISTRY AT WORK

Dear Rev. Dise:

I have been saved for a short time. I remember how I used to be when I wasn't saved, and so does everybody else, especially my husband. When I try to talk to him about the Lord, or invite him to church, he doesn't want to hear it, reminding me that I used to be just like him. I admit that I was like him at one time, but I am saved now. He accuses me of being holier than thou, and thinking that I am better than him. But I just want him to experience the joy that I am now feeling in the Lord. How do you witness to your loved ones without turning them away?

        Signed,

        New Christian

Dear New Christian:

Don't be discouraged about witnessing to your loved ones. Often the one who puts up the greatest resistance, is in fact, under conviction of the Holy Spirit. Let me suggest several considerations when witnessing.

Jesus said, "let your light so shine before men that they may see your good works and glorify your Father which is in heaven". (Matthew 5:16) To your family, you are what you have always been until you convince them otherwise. The convincing will begin when you show them you are a changed person... when you let your light shine. It is difficult for a person who has never experienced salvation, to believe that such a change is possible. So be patient. Don't expect them to accept what you say just because you said it.

Continue to witness to your boyfriend, family, and friends with love; not with contempt for their lifestyles. Remain optimistic. Believe in God's power to save no matter their initial reaction. Be patient and not pushy. It may take a while to convince them of the reality of a changed life. Keep witnessing by example first, and then by precept. Pray that you will be a good example and never stop praying that they will become believers.

RESOURCES

Carlson, Carole C. *Corrie ten Boom, Her life, Her faith.* Old Tappan, New Jersey: Fleming H. Revell Co., 1986. p. 129D.

Elliott, Elizabeth. *The Shaping of a Christian Family.* Ada, MI. Baker/Revell Pbl, 2000.

Gower, Ralph. *The New Manners & Customs of Bible Times.* Chicago, IL: Moody Press, 1987.

Graham, Stephany D. "Faith Power." in Hollies, Linda H. (Ed.) *Sister to Sister Devotions, Vol. Two.* Valley Forge, PA: Judson Press, 1999. pp. 94–95.

Hiscox, Edward T. *Star Book for Ministers.* Valley Forge, PA: The Judson Press, 1967.

Massey, James E. *The Worshiping Church: A Guide to the Experience of Worship.* Anderson, IN: Warner Press, 1961.

Unger, Merrill F. *Unger's Bible Dictionary.* Chicago, IL: Moody Press, 1983.

Winik, Lyric Wallwork. "When the Call Comes Later in Life." *Parade* magazine, October 1999, p. 3.

Additional Resources

Holy Bible, NIV, KJV

Johnnie Mae George Counseling & Prayer Manual (unpublished)

www.ingramcontent.com/pod-product-compliance
Lightning Source LLC
Chambersburg PA
CBHW060424010526
44118CB00017B/2345